A SHORT GUIDE
to WRITING
ABOUT HISTORY

A SHORT GUIDE to WRITING ABOUT HISTORY

■ ■ ■

Ninth Edition

RICHARD MARIUS
Late, Harvard University

MELVIN E. PAGE
East Tennessee State University

PEARSON

Boston   Columbus   Indianapolis   New York   San Francisco
Upper Saddle River   Amsterdam   Cape Town   Dubai   London   Madrid
Milan   Munich   Paris   Montreal   Toronto   Delhi   Mexico City   São Paulo
Sydney   Hong Kong   Seoul   Singapore   Taipei   Tokyo

Senior Sponsoring Editor: Katharine Glynn
Executive Marketing Manager: Roxanne McCarley
Project Manager: Rebecca Gilpin
Project Coordination, Text Design, and Electronic Page
    Makeup: Integra Software Services Private Ltd.
Creative Art Director: Jayne Conte
Cover Designer: Suzanne Duda
Cover Photo: Washington, D.C. March on Washington on August 28, 1963
    by Fred Ward BlackStart Photos/Newscom
Senior Manufacturing Buyer: Roy L. Pickering, Jr.
Printer/Binder: Edwards Brothers
Cover Printer: Lehigh-Phoenix

Credits and acknowledgments borrowed from other sources and reproduced, with permission, in this textbook appear on pages 182–183.

Library of Congress Cataloging-in-Publication Data
Marius, Richard.
    A short guide to writing about history / Richard Marius, Late, Harvard University, Melvin E. Page, East Tennessee State University.—Ninth edition.
    pages cm.
Includes bibliographical references and index.
ISBN-13: 978-0-321-95329-2 (alk. paper)
ISBN-10: 0-321-95329-0 (alk. paper)
    1. Historiography.   2. History—Research.   3. Academic writing.
    I. Page, Melvin E. (date),   II. Title.
D13.M294 2015
907—dc23
                                                    2013039921

10 9 8 7 6 5 4 3 2 1—EB—18 17 16 15 14

PEARSON

Student ISBN 10:   0-321-95329-0
Student ISBN 13: 978-0-321-95329-2

For our children—
Richard, Fred, and John
Megan, Melanie, and Michael
And our adventures together exploring history,
at home and around the world.

CONTENTS

■ ■ ■

PREFACE

∎ ∎ ∎

Since its first edition, thousands of college students have used *A Short Guide to Writing about History* to assist them in the process of writing history papers. This text shows students how to go beyond reporting the basic dates and facts of their history books and explains to them how to infuse their writing with their own ideas and unique perspective. In fact, this text was written to serve as an ideal complement for any history course intended to teach students to think and write like historians.

The text's original author, Professor Marius, pointed out in an early preface the misconceptions many students have about historical writing.

> Most students came into my courses believing that history was hardly more than a collection of names and dates to be memorized and repeated on examinations. They thought they could go to the library, look up several articles in encyclopedias, and write a paper to show how much they knew about a subject. They did not imagine that they could think for themselves about the facts.... It was my job to teach them that history becomes most exciting when we study a collection of primary sources—the basic stuff from which history is made—to make sense of these sources and tell a story about them.... Teaching people to write about history has been for me a means of showing students of all ages that they have worthwhile thoughts and can use them to write interesting and original essays on many subjects.

In creating the ninth edition, I have returned to Professor Marius's advice. We shared a passion about the study and writing of history and a great faith in the intelligence, tenacity, and curiosity of our students.

WHAT'S NEW IN THIS EDITION

- **Emphasis on new technologies.** This ninth edition continues to encourage the essential integration of electronic technologies into the work of historians. New developments in the use of digital books and journals as well as newly developed electronic note-taking programs are featured in the ninth edition, particularly their adaptation to smart phone and tablet computing applications.

- **Updated section on quantitative data and history.** The increasingly important role of using statistical analysis in historical research has been integrated into the ninth edition.

- **New section on scientific evidence.** With growing recognition among historians of the value scientific evidence bears on some historical problems, the ninth edition for the first time offers advice about using forensic science and other fields of study in historical essays.

- **Updated principles of note-taking.** In an effort to provide more direct guidance, which might serve to reduce the possibilities of accidental plagiarism, the principles for note-taking have been refined and clarified. The need to avoid copying full-text quotations is featured, not only in the principles but at other points in the ninth edition.

- **Renewed emphasis on Turabian citations.** All sample citations are updated to reflect suggestions from the new eighth edition of Kate L. Turabian, *A Manual for Writers of Research Papers, Theses, and Dissertations*, published in 2013. This also includes additional examples for making citations to electronic sources as well as other types of sources that sometimes present difficulties in notes and bibliographies.

- **Writing for presentations section.** For the first time this edition presents special consideration of writing for spoken reports, as well as advice on integrating visual elements into oral presentations.

- **Expanded bibliography.** The bibliography of student resources includes more sources, especially new titles that have been published in the past two years.

As before, I am eager to hear from readers about experiences with this book. Please write to me with any thoughts or questions you have about *A Short Guide to Writing About History*. Letters may be sent by post to me at the History Department, East Tennessee State University, Johnson City, TN 34614. You may also write using my e-mail address, pagem@etsu.edu. As did Professor Marius, I shall always respond.

ACKNOWLEDGMENTS

A number of historians at various colleges and universities offered priceless advice in the preparation of the manuscript for various editions of *A Short Guide to Writing About History*. I am particularly grateful to those whose thoughtful comments helped shape this ninth edition: Andrea Arrington, University of Arkansas; Jennifer M. Morris, College of Mount St. Joseph; Wesley Swanson, San Joaquin Delta College.

For this new edition I am grateful for the collaboration of a young colleague, Professor Brian J. Maxson. He has read the manuscript with a careful eye on the latest developments not only in historical research and writing, but also on the latest technologies that might serve to enhance the process of writing about history. Seeking the advice and counsel of a historian whose career is taking shape within the contemporary dynamics of the profession has aided me immeasurably in framing this ninth edition. As Professor Maxson shares the same vision of our students' potential that motivated both Richard Marius and me, his contributions to this new edition are especially welcome.

I also appreciate the support I have had from colleagues at three universities where I have taught about historical writing and research: Murray State University; Kenyatta University, Nairobi (Kenya); the University of Natal, Durban (South Africa); and East Tennessee State University. While all my colleagues have influenced my thinking about these subjects in one way or another over many years, in thinking about this edition I have especially appreciated conversations with my ETSU colleagues Dale Schmitt, Tom Lee, Steve Nash, and especially Brian Maxson on many details concerning historical writing and research. As always, I have also learned much from my students who shared with me their frustrations and triumphs in writing about history: Colleen Vasconsellos, Justin Horton, Bill Hembrock, Brandy Arnall, Kim Woodring, Kelley Hatch-Draper, Ron McCall, and my first "Kindle generation" undergraduates, especially Jeremy Williams, Michael Gilly, and Josh Ely. I particularly want to thank my former student Penny Sonnenburg-Willis for help in shaping my ideas and advice concerning research and note-taking. At Pearson Education, I appreciate the continued encouragement and confidence of Katharine Glynn and Rebecca Gilpin. And I would be remiss should I not mention the ongoing encouragement and assistance of my wife Grace as I worked on the ninth edition.

As I have written before, this edition, too, would not be possible without the road laid down by Richard Marius years ago. Collaborators such as he are hard to find. I continue to count myself fortunate, indeed.

MELVIN E. PAGE

A SHORT GUIDE
to WRITING
ABOUT HISTORY

WRITING AND HISTORY

■ ■ ■

After studying this chapter, you should be able to
- Create puzzles to begin historical stories.
- Appreciate writing as a way of thinking about history.
- Understand the five basic principles of history essays.
- Write paraphrases to avoid plagiarism.

Students struggling over an essay in history—for a book review, a full research paper, an examination, or even a short class assignment—have often told us that they know the subject, but they cannot write about it. In our experience this often means they have a jumble of facts and information in their heads but cannot tell a story about them.

Their complaint represents a discovery: History *does* involve telling a story, and while facts are essential in telling a story, they are not enough. If you know what armies faced each other, at what place, and who emerged victorious, you may not necessarily be able to tell a story about the encounter. Even if you know the names of the opposing commanders, and the various units under their command, it still may not be enough. Stories have tension, and while battles certainly have enough of that, you will need to sketch out the specific elements of that tension before readers will be engaged by your story. Why were the armies fighting each other? What were their expectations should they emerge victorious? Answering such questions also involves making reasoned arguments about the facts. And in doing so, you will help readers see the tensions, embrace the accounts of the struggle, and read on to see how it all comes out, not just who won and lost, but the implications of that outcome.

STORIES ABOUT THE PAST INTENDED TO BE TRUE

In writing about history, you tell the story of your thinking about a topic and formulate a central argument—or *thesis*—to say that things happened in a particular way and not another. You allow for the possibility that if this or this, or that, did *not* happen, things could have turned out entirely differently. And you explain what resulted from the events unfolding as they did.

Historians are like most people: They want to know what events mean, why they were important to what came afterward, and why we still talk about them. Like journalists, they ask *who, what, where, when,* and *why.* Who was responsible? What happened? Where did it happen? When and in what order did things happen? Why did they happen? And often historians ask additional questions, such as: What have other historians said about the event? What mistakes did they make that we can now correct? Historians are curious and relentless questioners, and the questions they ponder arise from any number of sources. All historical writing begins as an effort to answer questions about origins, happenings, and consequences. Historians find a puzzle and try to solve it. When you write for a history course, you must do the same—find a problem that stirs your curiosity and try to solve it. If you don't have a problem, you don't have a historical essay!

Consider these excerpts from the opening paragraphs of an article in *The American Historical Review,* the leading journal for historians in the United States. Notice how the author, Professor James Grehan, clearly states the puzzle he found, which prompted this essay.

> In April 1699, an unusual disturbance broke out in the streets of Cairo. As part of the annual pilgrimage caravan, which escorted Muslim pilgrims through the Sinai Desert to the holy cities of Arabia, a solemn procession was conveying a new silk covering destined for the Ka'ba, or Sacred Shrine, in Mecca. Among the most notable participants were a group of North Africans, who created an uproar as they moved through the streets. Fired by religious zeal, they insisted on applying their own brand of Islamic morality to the crowd of onlookers. In choosing targets for chastisement, they were very specific, beating all the people whom they found smoking tobacco. As the tumult grew, they made their decisive mistake. Seizing a member of a local paramilitary group, they smashed his pipe, and during the ensuing quarrel, went so far as to hit him over the head. The crowd

had apparently seen enough. Even as soldiers rushed to the scene, the "people of the marketplace" took matters into their own hands and began attacking the North Africans. The violence ended only with the arrival of a Janissary officer, who hauled the North Africans off to prison!

Looking back on this incident from a very different time and place, with our own concerns and passions about tobacco, it is hard not to be struck by the deep emotions that smoking, even then, was capable of eliciting. Walking around Middle Eastern towns today, one could never imagine that such struggles ever took place. Nearly everyone has now accepted smoking as a public freedom. Few people would dream of condemning it as a moral scourge, or of banishing it from the streets and markets…. This tolerant consensus did not emerge all at once. After its first arrival in the Ottoman Middle East at the end of the sixteenth century, tobacco would ignite intense debates about its legality and morality. The altercation in the streets of Cairo highlights these divisions of opinion….

Why had tobacco become the subject of such bitter controversy?[1]

Solving such puzzles of history involves both science and art. Science is a synonym for knowledge. But knowledge of what? History includes data—evidence, the names of people and places, when things happened, where they happened, bits of information gathered from many sources. It also includes interpretations of historians and others in the past who have written on the topic that the writer decides to treat in an essay. The art of history lies in combining fact and interpretation to tell a story about the past, as Professor Grehan did in his article.

Historians believe it is important to distinguish between the true and the false. Thus their stories, as the late Professor J. H. Hexter was fond of saying, are a "patterned, coherent account of the human past intended to be true,"[2] as distinguished from the fiction of novels and short stories, for example. In the sixteenth century some English writers called history "authentic stories" to distinguish it from fantastic tales about the past. Historians in the Renaissance searched for old documents, studied them to see if they were authentic, weeded out forgeries, and compared copies

---

[1]James Grehan, "Smoking and 'Early Modern' Sociability: The Great Tobacco Debate in the Ottoman Middle East (Seventeenth to Eighteenth Centuries)," *The American Historical Review* 111 (2006): 1352. We have omitted Professor Grehan's footnotes.

[2]J. H. Hexter, *The History Primer* (New York: Basic Books, 1971), 5.

to find errors scribes had made in transmitting texts. They also compared different stories told about the same events. These historians tried to tell the truth—just as historians do today.

But in the study of history, "truth" is complicated, contradictory, and often obscure. Every historical event happens one time and becomes separated from the present by the steady accumulation of other events happening day by day. We cannot put any incident from the past into a laboratory and make it happen again and again as we might conduct an experiment in chemistry, measuring and calculating to see precisely the relations of cause and effect. Instead, we must rely on evidence from the past such as memories of those who were there and objects from that time to guide us as we tell the story. But all these are mere records, subject to many interpretations and subject also to the tricks memory plays even on eyewitnesses. We can never relive the event *exactly* as it happened.

The evidence for past events is therefore always incomplete and fragmentary. Many pieces of evidence are lost, and others are often faded and warped. Historians fit the pieces together as carefully as possible, but holes remain in the picture they try to reconstruct. They do their best to fill in the holes with inferences that seem plausible and that fit the available facts. What emerges may closely resemble what happened, but we can never be completely sure that what we know as history is an exact replica of the past. Our knowledge of history is always in flux, and historians are always in dialogue, not only with the primary sources of the events they write about but also with other historians of those events.

In fact, for many historians this process is nothing less than an ongoing conversation, centered first on the use of evidence. "Only the use of footnotes" Anthony Grafton has asserted, since they offer citations of sources and sometimes commentary as well, "enables historians to make their texts not monologues but conversations."[3] Historians engage the evidence and commune with the sources, drawing out what is possible and then sharing the results with readers. The Australian humanist-historian Greg Dening was convinced of an even more crucial component: "Reading is my conversation with the world." For Dening, this inspired further engagement with the past, because "there is always another sentence to be added to the

---

[3]Anthony Grafton, *The Footnote: A Curious History* (Cambridge, MA: Harvard University Press, 1977), 234.

conversation,…another slant on the story."[4] You, too, can join in this conversation as you think about becoming a historian and begin writing about the past.

WRITING HISTORY AS A WAY OF THINKING

History and writing are inseparable. We cannot know history well unless we write about it. Writing allows us to arrange events and our thoughts, study our work, weed out contradictions, get names and places right, and question interpretations—our own and those of other historians. In writing we work out the chronological order of events—not a simple task but one indispensable to the historian's craft. Fluent talkers, on the other hand, can touch on first one idea and then another, sometimes using body language to stress a point. They can overwhelm opposition by charisma or by shouting when their argument is weak. Writers perform a more daring act! They must develop an idea with logic and clarity, knowing that a reader can study their words again and again and discover whether the words add up to a plausible argument, given the evidence available. If writers are illogical, unfair, untruthful, confused, or foolish, their words lie on the page to be attacked by anyone with the care and interest to look. Good talkers can contradict themselves, waffle, and weasel, and on being called to task, can claim that their hearers misunderstood them. Writers, however, must strive to be clear, logical, and fair, or they will be found out.

Good historical writing begins with the tension between what historical figures did and what they might have done. Herbert Butterfield, a respected philosopher of history, wrote that "history deals with the drama of human life as the affair of individual personalities, possessing self-consciousness, intellect, and freedom."[5] As drama, every part of the past has a unique quality. Every event we study in history existed in its own network of cause and effect, its own set of relations between people and events, its own modes of thought, usually taken for granted by the societies themselves, often assumed to be a divine ordination that could not be changed. A thunderstorm roars over the Kansas prairie today, and the unflappable television

---

[4]Greg Dening, "Performing on the Beaches of the Mind: An Essay," *History and Theory* 41 (2002): 3–7, http://www.jstor.org/stable/3590841.

[5]Herbert Butterfield, *Christianity and History* (New York: Scribner's, 1950), 26.

meteorologist explains that the storm is the result of a collision between a cold front and a warm front. In ancient Mesopotamia, the Babylonians heard in the thunder the voice of their god Marduk and thought that he was hurling lightning bolts into the earth. In these and countless other ways, spontaneous responses to many experiences in the past were different from those of the present day. Part of the historian's task is to think your way into the minds of the people who lived in earlier times so you can think about experiences as they did. That's where your historical conversations begin.

You can never fully abandon your own perceptions, nor recover the past exactly as people then thought of life and the world. Historians must always put something of themselves into the stories they tell; never are they empty vessels through which the records of the past spew forth as if they were an untouched truth about the past. This inevitable insertion of the historian into historical accounts is what J. H. Hexter called an application of "the second record," encompassing "everything which historians bring to their confrontation with the record of the past."[6] While this is an inevitable legacy of the historian's work, it is one which must always be kept in check lest the stories that emerge lose any semblance of credulity. And that is a crucial test: Are the stories, as well as the explanations and analysis they offer, credible? And are they, as Greg Dening put it, "honest to the realities of living, experiential, recognizably human"?[7] In short, will they draw more people into the conversation?

Sometimes credulity and "the realities of living" undermine historians' assumptions, such as long-standing notions which focused historical accounts almost entirely on what men did. If women entered the story, it was because they did things male historians generally expected men to do. They ruled countries, as did Queen Elizabeth I of England; they refined radium, as Marie Curie did in France; they wrote novels, as did Shikibu Murasaki in eleventh-century Japan. Now historians are turning to many other areas of historical interest. A random glance through recent issues of *The American Historical Review* will show discussions such as Catherine Kudlick's review essay on "Disability History: Why We Need Another 'Other,'"[8] as well as the work of many other skilled female historians. Articles such as Barbara Metcalf's "Islam and Power in Colonial India: The Making and Unmaking

---

[6]Hexter, 79.

[7]Dening, 4.

[8]Catherine J. Kudlick, "Disability History: Why We Need Another 'Other,'" *The American Historical Review* 108 (2003): 763–793.

of a Muslim Princess"[9] provide insights into topics that conventional male historians of a century ago dismissed as irrelevant, but that today occupy an honored and fascinating place in serious historical research. In a most striking way, the memoir of the distinguished African American historian John Hope Franklin, *Mirror to America*, provides similar evidence of both the subjects of contemporary history and the growing diversity among historians.[10] Still others write of the history of immigrants, labor history, sexual history, and the history of fashion or sport. All these and more demonstrate the diverse interests of historians toiling to uncover as much of the human experience as possible.

Whatever its subject, the study of history is an unending detective story. Historians try to solve puzzles in the evidence and to tell a story that will give order to the confusion of data we inherit from the past. Historians make connections, assign causes, trace defects, make comparisons, uncover patterns, locate dead ends, and find influences that continue through the generations until the present. And in doing so they apply their minds to the sources and their considered judgments to the evidence, writing those stories about the past they intend to be both credible and true.

You, too, encounter history by reading, and by your own writing as well. By reading books and articles, you slowly gain some understanding of the shape of the past, the general framework within which events took place. And as you read what other historians have written, you will also develop a storehouse of knowledge about historical writing, which you can draw upon to improve your own essays. Writing helps all of us think about what we know, and of course it helps your instructors see what you know and how you think. In your history courses you may be asked to write brief essays of perhaps only one or two pages, either as homework assignments or during class, frequently reflecting on some assigned reading. Sometimes your writing will take the form of essay answers to questions on exams. Occasionally you might be asked to review a history book, either one that you select or one that is assigned to you. And often you may also be expected to prepare longer papers, which will require you to conduct research in your own college library, on the Internet, and elsewhere as well.

---

[9]Barbara Metcalf, "Islam and Power in Colonial India: The Making and Unmaking of a Muslim Princess," *The American Historical Review* 116 (2011): 1–30.

[10]John Hope Franklin, *Mirror to America* (New York: Farrar, Straus, and Giroux, 2005).

Even though your writing about the past will take a number of forms, some basic principles apply to writing any history essay. Perhaps the most important is that thinking about the past is the key to writing history and entering into the ongoing historical conversation. Thus this is a book about both methods of historical study and methods in writing. It should help you gain some understanding of general problems underlying all historical study, and it should help your writing in all your college or university courses. It should also make you a better detective and a better teller of some of the innumerable stories that taken together make up the study of the past. We will discuss research you can conduct in your own college library or on the Internet and also include a brief section about how to take notes on your reading and research. Our emphasis will be on how to use those notes and your acquired knowledge to do well on research papers, on shorter essays, and on examinations you may write in a history course.

BASIC PRINCIPLES FOR HISTORY ESSAYS

Obviously, history is far more than an assembly of facts about what happened in the past. It is the writer's interpretation of facts that raises questions, provokes curiosity, and makes us ask the questions *who*, *what*, *where*, *when*, and *why*. The writer's interpretation should concentrate on a central argument, or *thesis*, that binds everything in an essay together. No matter what kind of essay you are writing, once you have developed the thesis that will tie the entire essay together, there are five key principles which can help you in examining your own writing to see if it conforms to the expectations that readers—including your instructors—bring to their reading of history essays. Don't disappoint them. Guide your own writing by the following standards.

1. Good historical essays are sharply focused on a limited topic.

You can develop a thrill of historical discovery *only* if your topic is sufficiently limited to let you study and think about the sources carefully. If you are able to choose your own topic, select one you can manage in the time and space you have available; this is true for writing essay test responses as well as papers that allow you more time to develop your thoughts. Sometimes your instructor may assign a topic for your essay. Usually, such prescribed topics are already sharply focused, but even if they are not, you can usually find ways to limit the essay you prepare.

Historians often use specific research to explore broader questions, as you can see in Charles Ambler's essay in *The American Historical Review* on "Popular Films and the Colonial Audience: The Movies in Northern Rhodesia." Professor Ambler begins very specifically:

> During the 1940s and 1950s, no visitor to the coppermining cities of the colonial Northern Rhodesia (Zambia) in central Africa could escape the visible marks of the impact of American films. In the vast company compounds that housed the African miners and their families on the Copperbelt, groups of African boys, "dressed in home-made paper 'chaps' and cowboy hats, and carrying crudely carved wooden pistols," were a ubiquitous presence running through the streets and alleys in endless games of cowboys and Indians. Others appeared "more sinister,... with a black mask over the eyes and a wooden dagger in the belt." As they engaged in their mock battles, they could be heard shouting, "Jeke, Jeke," a local corruption of "Jack," the universal term among urban moviegoers in the British central African colonies for the heroes of cowboy films. In the same streets, young men affected styles of dress that plainly showed the influence of westerns and gangster films—ten-gallon hats, kerchiefs, and so forth.
>
> This phenomenon of "Copperbelt Cowboys" and its manifestation in urban areas across much of British-ruled Africa vividly demonstrates the rapid and pervasive penetration of mythic Hollywood screen imagery into even remote corners of the empire.

Professor Ambler, however, is careful in his next paragraph to make certain his readers appreciate that the specific focus of his essay serves a broader historical purpose, since it "takes up the history of film entertainment in Northern Rhodesia in order to explore the broad question of the transmission and reception of Western mass culture in the context of colonialism."[11] This is precisely the sort of technique that you can use to focus your essays. Rather than trying to write about an almost hopelessly broad subject, limit yourself to a more specific topic that can help

---

[11]Charles Ambler, "Popular Films and Colonial Audiences: The Movies in Northern Rhodesia," *The American Historical Review* 106 (2001): 81–82. We have omitted Professor Ambler's citations of his sources.

address the larger issues. There is a lesson here for any young historian: If you try to do too much, you will not do anything. Often discussing your essays, and especially your longer papers, with your instructor will be a valuable aid in helping you focus your writing appropriately.

Keeping your focus clear should also lead you to a conclusion that will mirror the points you made as you began your essay. Once you have introduced the puzzle you wish to consider, you should clearly tell the story that will engage your readers. But writers of history essays should not work toward surprise endings!

Inexperienced writers often fall into the temptation to withhold necessary information or otherwise distract readers to prevent them from guessing where the story is going. Such tactics are annoying, and professional historians do not use them. The climax in a history paper is usually a place where the last block of information is fitted in place and the writer's case is proved as well as his or her knowledge permits. The paper closes shortly after the climax because once the case is proved, a summary of the significance of the events or ideas reflecting how the essay began is all that is necessary.

For example, once Professor Ambler presents the story of cinema and its influence in Northern Rhodesia, he comes to the climax and then quickly finishes by returning to the points he made in the beginning of his essay:

> In postcolonial Zambia, the introduction of television and more recently the proliferation of small video dens and individually owned video-cassette recorders has effectively pushed the bioscope—formal film showings—to the margins of entertainment. The current popularity of martial arts and other contemporary action movies has overshadowed the deep affection for the cowboy genre exhibited by several generations of viewers in the industrial towns of the Copperbelt and elsewhere in east, central, and southern Africa. But if the encounter of African audiences with film in the 1940s and 1950s lacked the complexity of the diverse and fragmented circulation of media that is characteristic of Zambia and the rest of southern Africa today, it is apparent that the critical process through which audiences consume visual media developed on a diet of horse operas.[12]

Of course, coordinating the beginning and end of your essay without careful attention to what comes between will not be sufficient to impress

---

[12]Ambler, 105.

your readers. Any good piece of writing leads you through a process of discovery, providing information that lets you follow the writer's lead, finally arriving at the climax where everything comes together. Readers not only want to know how things come out but also how they happen.

2. Historical essays should have a clearly stated argument.

Historians write essays to interpret something they want readers to know about the past. They provide data—information from their sources—and their argument about what that evidence means. Here, *argument* does not mean angry, insulting debate as though anyone who disagrees with you is a fool; that would be counterproductive for any conversation! Rather, it is the main thing the writer wants to tell readers, the reason for writing the essay. It is the *thesis* of the essay, the proposition that the writer wants readers to accept. Don't be content with telling a story others have told hundreds of time, the sort of story you might copy out of an encyclopedia whose aim is to give you nothing but the facts. Find something puzzling in the evidence, and try to solve the puzzle or to explain why it is a puzzle. Ask a question and try to answer it. But get to the point straightaway.

A good essay sets the scene quickly, reveals a tension to be resolved, and sets out in the direction of a solution. Some writers take so long to introduce their essays that readers lose interest before they get to the writer's real beginning. They may shovel out piles of background information or long accounts of previous scholarship in a somewhat frantic effort to prove that the writer has studied the issue. Or they may give some sort of moral justification for the topic, as if to say they are on the side of righteousness. The best writers have something to say and start saying it quickly. Readers should know your general subject in the first paragraph, and by the next paragraph they should usually know why you have written your essay and the argument you wish to make.

Consider the opening paragraphs of Professor Leora Auslander's essay in a recent issue of *The American Historical Review*. She quickly makes clear the problem she sees in the usual practice of historians and then moves directly to her thesis:

> Historians are, by profession, suspicious of things. Words are our stock-in-trade. This is not to say, of course, that historians have never had recourse to non-linguistic sources. From the use of archaeological

evidence in the nineteenth century to Marc Bloch's brilliant notion that the intricacies of medieval landholding patterns could be deciphered by observing the interwar French countryside from a small plane, historians have looked beyond the holdings of archives and libraries. Scholars of the ancient, medieval, and early modern worlds, and of science and technology—those whose written sources are limited or whose very object is material—have pushed the evidentiary boundaries the furthest, although some modernists and social and cultural historians have also used visual, material, and musical sources. Despite these initiatives, however, most historians view words as the most trustworthy as well as the most informative sources; everything else is merely illustrative or supplementary.

I will argue here, by contrast, that expanding the range of our canonical sources will provide better answers to familiar historical questions as well as change the very nature of the questions we are able to pose and the kind of knowledge we are able to acquire about the past. Each form of human expression has its unique attributes and capacities; limiting our evidentiary base to one of them—linguistic—renders us unable to grasp important dimensions of human experience, and our explanations of major historical problems are thereby impoverished. Within the category of the extralinguistic, I will make an argument for the utility and importance of material culture in particular.[13]

Her second paragraph begins with her thesis, which she then explains by outlining some of the argument she will make in her essay.

Make careful note of this example. Once you have begun your essay, don't digress. Stick to the point. Be sure everything in your essay serves your main purpose, and be sure your readers understand the connection to your main purpose of everything you include. Don't imagine that you have to put everything you know into one essay. An essay makes a point. It is not an excuse to pour out facts as if you were dumping the contents of a can onto a tabletop. As Auslander writes in her conclusion, historians must have a commitment "to the goal of understanding, interpreting, and perhaps even explaining the world beyond the text or the object."[14] And as her essay demonstrates, even as historians look for "extralinguistic" evidence, they must *write* clearly about their conclusions.

---

[13]Leora Auslander, "Beyond Words," *The American Historical Review* 110 (2005): 1015.

[14]Auslander, 1045.

3. Historical essays are built, step by step, on carefully acknowledged evidence.

You must also give readers reasons to believe your story. Your readers must accept you as an authority for the essay you present to them. You cannot write history off the top of your head, and you cannot parade your opinions unless you support them. To do that you must command your evidence, present it clearly and carefully, and fully acknowledge where you have found it. But what is evidence? The issue is complicated. Evidence is detailed factual information from primary and secondary sources. But those distinctions are measured not by what the source is, but by what you are writing about. Primary sources are those closest, in time or connection, to any subject of investigation. They could be written, created, or used by the subjects you are writing about. Secondary sources, however, are always written *about* primary sources.

For example, primary sources for an essay about the Mexican revolutionary Emiliano Zapata early in the twentieth century would be letters, speeches, and other writings of Zapata himself, and perhaps also objects he owned or created. Secondary sources would be books and articles by scholars such as John Womack and Samuel Brunk, who have made careers of studying Zapata's movement and his assassination. Always keep in mind that good essays and papers are based on primary sources; so for such a topic you would consider not only the works of Professors Womack and Brunk, but if at all possible those of Zapata himself.

In writing a research essay, you must sift through all the available sources you can, both primary and secondary, decide what is reliable and what is not, what is useful and what is not, and how you will use these sources in your work. And in writing shorter essays, such as those on exams, you must keep in mind what evidence you have learned about and mention it. When you make a generalization, immediately support it by quoting, paraphrasing, summarizing, or otherwise referring to a source. Generalizations are unconvincing without the help of specific evidence to give them content.

Evidence is everywhere. The letters and papers of women and men, famous and obscure, make fascinating records of their times, as do collections of their belongings frequently housed in museums, large and small. Many collections of such evidence, from the classical age to the present, have been published in written and photographic form and presented in print or online. You can pick a subject and follow the writer's thoughts and other expressions on it, or about events related to the subject, and have an excellent paper for a college history course. Similarly, newspapers (many are preserved in microform or digital formats) often provide exceptional insights into the past, which may stimulate your curiosity and help you formulate the sorts of puzzles that make for good historical essays. They may also provide significant details to supplement the other sources available to you.

Sources of local history abound in courthouses, privately held diaries and letters, tax records, city directories, and myriad other records. These sources can provide details, often small ones, which can make the past come alive in a moment. And never forget the power of the interview in writing about history. If you write about any historical event of the past fifty or sixty years, often with a little effort you can find somebody who participated in it. Participants frequently may be delighted to share their stories with you. And their stories can illuminate major social movements in the country as a whole. You may also find transcripts of previous interviews in local history publications, newspapers, or archive collections, and occasionally available online. But always remember that participants can get things wrong, either in their interviews or in what they might have written about their experiences. Human beings forget, or they tell the story in such a way to exalt themselves, and sometimes they simply lie. As a careful questioner, the historian is always skeptical enough to check out the stories, even from eyewitnesses. In doing so, you frequently will confirm that secondary sources are also essential.

You should always consult books and articles written by historians about the subject you write about yourself. These books and articles will provide much information that you can use, especially if you seek out some of the sources those historians have relied upon. Perhaps more important, you will discover what other historians have thought about the problems you are investigating and how they have evaluated the same, or similar, primary sources as those you have found. Discovering this sort of historiographic evidence—how previous historians have written about your topic or issues closely related to it—can help you learn how to think about history generally. And that will assist you as well as in carefully selecting the most appropriate evidence from the vast amount available for a specific project and fit it together to create a story—an explanation, an argument. Carefully reading secondary sources will also help you see how historians document their sources by means of footnotes, endnotes, or attributions written into the text. Even as you write, however, remember you will only gain authority for your own work if you demonstrate that you are familiar with *both* the primary sources and the work of others who have studied the same material. But the confidence you develop by providing evidence for your points is only as good as the confidence your readers have in how you obtained it. If you make a careless summary of your evidence or simply get it wrong, you lose the respect of knowledgeable readers. The recent experience of one historian, Michael Bellesiles, is very instructive for any young historian.

Almost immediately after its publication in 2000, Professor Bellesiles's book, *Arming America: The Origins of a National Gun Culture*, was widely praised, and his thesis, that the American "gun culture" was a post–Civil War development, enmeshed him in political arguments with many who believe the importance of gun ownership in America is older than the Constitution. In the midst of that controversy, historians began to examine his use of evidence only to find much to question: inaccurate citations to archival holdings, misreading of documents, generalizations based on limited sampling of court records, and sloppy recording of his data. Although Professor Bellesiles made several statements in his defense, none proved sufficient to quiet the outcry, and trustees of the prestigious Bancroft Prize for historical writing withdrew the award they had originally given to him for the book.[15]

Bellesiles's sad experience should be instructive. Be certain that you take careful note of the sources you consult. It is important that you be clear in your notes about what you learned from which source, and that you quote correctly any material you copy directly from those sources. This is true not only for the notes you make from written sources, but also for those you obtain from increasingly widely available electronic resources. Both require special care.

As you begin writing about history, be careful to make appropriate citations for all the material from your sources that you mention in your essay. While it is widely accepted that historians need not always document matters of common knowledge, our advice is that you err on the side of caution by making appropriate citations for all the information from your sources you use in an essay. Your instructors will most likely appreciate your diligence. In a few cases you may develop ideas on your own that are not precisely the same as those you read in secondary sources. You should

---

[15]Several perspectives on this controversy may be found in a "*Forum: Historians and Guns*," *William and Mary Quarterly* 59 (2002): 203–268.

then document those secondary sources and, either in a footnote or in the body of your text, point out the similarities and the differences between those sources and what you have written.

4. Historical essays reflect the dispassionate thoughts of the author.

While you should take great care to acknowledge what previous historians have written about a topic, do not disappoint your readers by telling them only what other people have said about your subject. Try to show them that by reading your work, they will learn something new or see old knowledge in a new light, one that you have shed on the subject by your own study and thinking.

One of the saddest things we have found about teaching is the conviction of too many of our students that they have nothing fresh and interesting to say about their topics. They don't trust themselves. They cannot express a thought unless they have read it somewhere else. One reason for this lack of confidence is that some students insist on writing about large, general topics that other people have written about hundreds of times. Only a little searching in almost any college or university library will turn up evidence of topics that have seldom been written about. You may not find new facts, but you can think carefully about the facts at your disposal and come up with something fresh and interesting. You can see new relationships. You can see causes and effects and connections that others have missed. You may reflect on motives and influences. You may spot places where some sources are silent. You can present your own conclusions, based on the evidence you have accumulated, which have the weight of authority behind them.

Some students go to the library looking for information on a broad subject like the beginnings of the Civil War and take a piece of information here and another piece there. They stick it all together without contributing anything of their own except manual dexterity. They retell a story that has been told thousands of times, and they do not present a thought that they have not read elsewhere. Why not instead read the speech Senator Jefferson Davis of Mississippi made in the United States Senate as he resigned to become president of the Confederacy? You might explain in an essay his justification for secession—and see if you think he left something out. Then you have a thoughtful paper. Do not be happy until you shape a story that cannot be read in any encyclopedia or textbook in the field.

Offering your own original ideas does not mean that you should choke your prose with your own emotions. Historians identify with the people and the times they write about, and often in studying history emotions are aroused. In writing about the past, you judge people and decide whether they were good or bad. The best way to convey these judgments is to tell what these people did or said. You don't have to prove that you are on the side of the angels. You should trust your readers as you would a friend with whom you are conversing. If characters you describe did terrible things, readers can see the evil if you give them the details. If characters did noble things, your readers can tell that, too, without any emotional insistence on your part. Simply adopt the approach of all good historians by trying to tell the truth about what happened.

Of course, if you study any issue long enough and carefully enough, you will form opinions about it. You will think you know why something happened, or you will suppose that you understand someone. And you may develop strong personal views about the personalities or the outcome. Yet the evidence in history seldom stacks up entirely on one side of an issue, especially in the more interesting problems about the past. Different parts of the evidence can often contradict each other; using your own judgment about it all means that you must face such contradictions squarely. If you do not, knowledgeable readers may decide that you are careless, incompetent, or even dishonest. History is not a seamless garment. Knowledge of the past—or of almost anything else—has bumps and rips and blank spots that remain even when historians have done their best to put together a coherent account of it.

It is also true that different historians interpret the same data in different ways. So it is not unusual to find new and different interpretations of the past, sometimes including new evidence and sometimes rethinking what the well-known evidence means. This *revisionism* is hardly the dangerous approach to the past that is occasionally denounced in the press; rather, it is the normal work of writing history. Joyce Appleby, Lynn Hunt, and Margaret Jacob—the first two former presidents of the American Historical Association—have noted that historians "do not so much revise historical knowledge as they reinvest it with contemporary interest." [16] But they do so with care and consideration of other points of view. Consider this opening

---

[16]Joyce Appleby, Lynn Hunt, and Margaret Jacob, *Telling the Truth About History* (New York: W.W. Norton, 1994), 265.

paragraph by Camilla Townsend in her *American Historical Review* article, "Burying the White Gods: New Perspectives on the Conquest of Mexico":

> In 1552, Francisco López de Gómara, who had been chaplain and secretary to Hernando Cortés while he lived out his old age in Spain, published an account of the conquest of Mexico. López de Gómara himself had never been to the New World, but he could envision it nonetheless. "Many [Indians] came to gape at the strange men, now so famous, and at their attire, arms and horses, and they said, 'These men are gods!'" The chaplain was one of the first to claim in print that the Mexicans had believed the conquistadors to be divine. Among the welter of statements made in the Old World about the inhabitants of the New, this one found particular resonance. It was repeated with enthusiasm, and soon a specific version gained credence: the Mexicans had apparently believed in a god named Quetzalcoatl, who long ago had disappeared in the east, promising to return from that direction on a certain date. In an extraordinary coincidence, Cortés appeared off the coast in that very year and was mistaken for Quetzalcoatl by the devout Indians. Today, most educated persons in the United States, Europe, and Latin America are fully versed in this account, as readers of this piece can undoubtedly affirm. In fact, however, there is little evidence that the indigenous people ever seriously believed the newcomers were gods, and there is no meaningful evidence that any story about Quetzalcoatl's return from the east ever existed before the conquest. A number of scholars of early Mexico are aware of this, but few others are. The cherished narrative is alive and well, and in urgent need of critical attention.[17]

Professor Townsend's approach illustrates the very reasonable way historians bring new ideas of their own into an essay. You can do the same. You do not weaken your argument by recognizing different views. On the contrary, you strengthen your case by showing readers that you know what others have said, even if their opinions contradict your own. Readers will believe you if you deal with contrary opinions honestly, but they will scorn your work if you pretend that contradictions don't exist. This advice translates into a simple principle: Be honest, not arrogant. Nothing turns readers off so quickly as to suppose that the writer is not being fair.

---

[17]Camilla Townsend, "Burying the White Gods: New Perspectives on the Conquest of Mexico," *The American Historical Review* 108 (2003): 659.

5. History essays are clearly written with an intended audience in mind.

Readers are also turned off if they are distracted by asking questions like these as they read: Is that word spelled correctly? Why is a comma missing here? Does this word fit the context? Reading—like writing—is hard work, especially when the material is dense or complicated, as it often is in history courses. Readers want to pay attention to what a writer says. A careless attitude toward the conventions—among them common practices of grammar and punctuation—may not bother writers because they think they know what they want to say. But it throws readers off.

Students who complain when instructors enforce the conventions do themselves a great disservice. In the world beyond college, few things about your writing will be more harshly judged than careless disregard for the conventions. Most everyone would like to believe their ideas are so compelling that no one can resist them, no matter how sloppily they write. Readers you seek to impress in a job application, a report, or a letter will judge otherwise. But merely reading over our suggestions, or listening to others from your instructors, is not enough. You must actively apply them and others, such as those in Bryan A. Garner's excellent chapter in the new, sixteenth edition of *The Chicago Manual of Style*.[18]

In part, this means you should respect the audience for whom you are writing, the readers who will join you in the historical conversation that you have entered. So always consider what your intended audience already knows. Just as you convey to your readers an "implied author" in what you write, you should also write with an implied reader in mind, someone you think may read your work. For most history courses, you should write for your instructor and other students who are interested in your topic but may not be specialists in the field. Define important terms. Give enough information to provide a context for your essay. Say something about your sources, but do not get lost in background information that your readers know already. The best you can do is to imagine yourself as a reader and consider the sort of thing you might read and believe, and write accordingly.

---

[18]Bryan A. Garner, "Grammar and Usage," in *The Chicago Manual of Style*, 16th ed. (Chicago: University of Chicago Press, 2010), 201–304; several subsequent chapters on punctuation, spelling, and similar matters are also valuable for writers.

It is not always an easy task. The main principle is that you must always be making decisions about what you need to tell your readers and what you think they know already. For example, if you write an interpretation of Martin Luther King, Jr.'s *Letter from Birmingham Jail* of 1963, you will bore readers and even offend them if you write as if they have never heard of Dr. King. In the same way, you don't inform your readers that Shakespeare was an English playwright or that Nelson Mandela was the first black president of South Africa.

We tell our students that they should write their essays so that if a friend or spouse picked one up, they could read it with the same understanding and pleasure they might find in an article in a serious magazine. The essay should be complete in itself. The important terms should be defined. Everyone quoted or mentioned in the essay should be identified—unless someone is well known to the general public. All the necessary information should be included. Try to imagine that friend picking up your essay and not being able to stop until finishing the piece. And it is always a good idea to have some other person read your work and try to say back to you what he or she thinks you have said; such readers might also be able to suggest improvements in your writing!

Having someone read your essay and comment on it, however, does not change your own responsibility for proofreading your essay carefully. Read it over and over to find misspelled words, lapses in grammar, typos, and places where you have inadvertently left out a word (a common error in these days of writing with the computer). Use the spell checker (and grammar checker) on your word processing program. But remember! The computer cannot replace the brain, although it will often help you ask questions about your writing before your readers do.

These principles for a good essay should serve you well. Keep them in mind as you write your own history essays. This short, summary checklist will help you focus on them as you do.

Writer's Checklist of Basic Principles

_____ ✔ Have I narrowed my topic sufficiently?
_____ ✔ Do the first and last sections of my essay mirror each other?
_____ ✔ Do I have a clearly stated argument?
_____ ✔ Are my ideas on the subject clear?
_____ ✔ Is the evidence on which I based my essay clear?
_____ ✔ Have I documented my sources?

_____ ✔ Have I written dispassionately?

_____ ✔ Have I acknowledged other views?

_____ ✔ Have I written clearly, using common conventions of written English?

_____ ✔ Have I kept my intended audience in mind?

PARAPHRASE AND PLAGIARISM

Even if you are successful in following the basic principles for history essays, nothing will undermine your writing more than carelessness driven by haste or fear that you are inadequate for the task. The frequent result, *plagiarism*—presenting the thoughts or words of others as your own—is the ultimate dishonesty in writing. In recent years several well-known historians, including Doris Kearns Goodwin and the late Stephen Ambrose, have been forced to admit that due to their personal inattention, portions of several of their books were copied from the work of other writers. Claims of simple carelessness or exuberance in telling a story, such as those made by Professor Ambrose, are simply insufficient. Readers naturally expected better from him, and they will of you as well. Frequently authors who are challenged in court by those whose work they have appropriated and presented as their own face costly and embarrassing results. In any case such thefts of intellectual property are seldom forgotten.

These and other recent cases of plagiarism do not seem to have diminished such occurrences, even among our own students. Perhaps the issue of plagiarism seems little more than an inconsequential theoretical or moral dilemma to them, or they believe they will not be detected. Maybe they conclude that since some famous historians (such as Professor Goodwin) have continued their successful careers even after acknowledging such misdeeds, they will be able to escape serious consequences as well. A federal judge, Richard A. Posner, who wrote a short book about plagiarism a few years ago, concluded that students who plagiarize are driven to do so primarily by desires "to save time, to get better grades, or both."[19] Should you face similar dilemmas, keep in mind that at colleges and universities, the penalties for plagiarism are severe. Plagiarists frequently are summoned before a disciplinary board, sometimes expelled

---

[19]Richard A. Posner, *The Little Book of Plagiarism* (New York: Pantheon Books, 2007), 89.

for one or more terms of study, and usually the plagiarism is recorded permanently on their academic records. Almost never do the claims of those accused—that they did not understand the issue or were merely unaware of their transgressions—result in greater leniency.

Much better that you simply take steps to avoid any appearance of plagiarism. Your efforts to do so should begin even as you are taking notes from your sources. Take special care to record most of your notes in your own words. And *always* put material you copy directly from your sources in quotation marks in your notes and mark them as quotations. If you later use that information word for word in your essay as you found it in the sources—even if it is only a short phrase or brief sentence—put it in quotation marks in your essay as well, and make a clear citation to the source you are quoting. In addition, take care to use ellipses (. . .) when necessary for words you have deleted and brackets ([ ]) for any you have inserted in the quotation. It is especially important that you set aside your notes as you write, expressing ideas in your own words, only later going back to check what you have written with your notes and in your sources.

Also keep in mind that no matter how you keep notes, electronic research and writing advances come with associated dangers. In particular, the ease of "block and click" operations used to capture and move electronic text from one file (or even a Web page) to another can all too easily lead to including large segments of a source directly in your notes. If you use this technique, be certain to use quotation marks and also mark those notes as quotations. If you are careless, you will be guilty of plagiarism! Remember: It is *your* responsibility to avoid such errors.

Lest you slip into careless habits in using electronic—or any other—sources, you should be aware of the greatly increased use of *Turnitin* and similar services that allow you and your instructors to check the originality of your essays. Some colleges and universities use the service as a matter of campus policy, but it is also available for use by individual instructors. Even if you do not submit your essay through a *Turnitin* interface, your papers may be submitted directly by your instructor. Your work will be compared with most of the public Internet content, many subscription-based content providers (including writing-for-payment sites), as well as previous papers submitted to *Turnitin*. And there is also a considerable database of print sources used in making the comparisons. Reports on these comparisons—including side-by-side contrasts with the originals—are generated for your instructors and sometimes for you as well. Thus *Turnitin* provides a resource for the speedy checking of your work for originality.

Understanding the availability of such a service should serve as an encouragement for your careful efforts at original writing.

Our best advice is straightforward: You should always make certain that your essays are your own work and that you always give credit for ideas you get from someone else, even if you paraphrase or express those ideas in your own words. Heed the advice of Professor Peter Hoffer to paraphrase only "with great care...to avoid falling into plagiarism":

> Paraphrasing lends itself to a wide range of errors. In particular, a paraphrase...[made] in the course of research, may be mistaken by the author for his or her own idea or language and reappear in the author's piece without any attribution. Mosaic paraphrases patching together quotations from a variety of secondary sources, and close paraphrases, wherein the author changes a word or two and reuses a passage from another author without quotations marks, also constitute plagiarism.
>
> In print all paraphrases, no matter how long or how many works are paraphrased, must be followed by citations to the sources that are as clear and precise as those provided for a direct quotation.[20]

The process of paraphrasing and summarizing, however, is sometimes hard to grasp. The following example may help you see how to do so in your own research and writing, thus avoiding the problem of plagiarism. Here is a paragraph from a book by world historian Jerry Bentley:

> Beginning in the fifteenth century, and continuing to some extent to the present day, new configurations of technology and new patterns of disease favored Europeans in their dealings with nonwestern peoples. The technology in question was not absolutely new, nor was it always European in origin. Much of it traced ultimately to Tang and Song inventions: gunpowder, the compass, the stern-post rudder, and other elements of nautical technology all came ultimately from China. Other items also came from eastern parts, most notably the lanteen sail, which originated in the Indian Ocean and came to the Mediterranean through the agency of Arab merchants and mariners. The Europeans borrowed much of their naval and military technology, but they refined, accumulated, and combined it to the point that they at least matched and most

---

[20]Peter Charles Hoffer, "Reflections on Plagiarism—Part 1: 'A Guide for the Perplexed,'" *Perspectives: Newsmagazine of the American Historical Association* 42, no. 2 (February 2004): 19.

often exceeded the technological development of other peoples. When the Europeans ventured into the Atlantic Ocean in the fifteenth century, they not only possessed highly maneuverable vessels and the instruments necessary to chart their courses (at least approximately) and return safely but also drew upon an arsenal of powerful weapons that dismembered and profoundly disoriented people who had not before encountered such destructive machinery. Sophisticated naval and military technologies by no means provided Europeans with the means to dominate all the peoples they encountered—certainly not before the development of the steamboat and advanced weapons in the nineteenth century—but they underwrote western hegemony in the world over a very long term. [21]

And here is a way you could summarize this passage, using your own words as you might when paraphrasing:

> Jerry Bentley makes a strong case that European imperialism rested on technology. Most of the key inventions, in military and naval equipment, were borrowed and then both modified and enhanced by European craftsmen. These developments gave them a clear advantage over other peoples they encountered and then conquered. [21]

These ideas clearly come from Bentley's book, even though they do not directly quote him. In making such a summary, you *must* make a citation to Bentley's work saying, in effect, this is where I got these ideas. In this example, note that the citations we have included are exactly the same for the quotation and also the paraphrase. Citations to your own restatement of ideas, whether from secondary or even primary sources, will usually be much more common in your essays than ones documenting a direct quotation. That is, you will paraphrase or summarize much more frequently than you quote directly. Be certain that you do so with care!

Sometimes student writers will conclude that simply using lots of quotations and many footnotes or endnotes is all that is necessary to ensure they will not be guilty of inadvertent plagiarism. Such caution is a step

---

[21]Jerry H. Bentley, *Old World Encounters* (New York: Oxford University Press, 1993), 183.

in the right direction but can also diminish the quality of their writing. You should always keep direct quotations to a minimum, using them only when they serve an essential purpose in your essays. And documentation of your sources, while clearly important, should also be kept to the minimum necessary for careful attribution. Following the advice of some writing experts, some students also make use of signal phrases when beginning the presentation of quotations ("Lincoln said") or ideas ("As Richard Hofstadter discusses in his book") or following quotations ("as Linda Kerber has written"). These, too, can be overused and sometimes seem stilted, but they can be successful in indicating how you have used your sources. However, you must still use appropriate citations for all the information you identify with signal phrases.

Keep in mind that you also need to follow all the basic principles for history essays as you finish your writing efforts. Then you can refer to these questions as you double-check your efforts to avoid plagiarism:

Writer's Checklist for Avoiding Plagiarism

_____ ✔ Are all quotations in the notes from my research clearly marked?

_____ ✔ Have I taken care to separate my own ideas in my research notes?

_____ ✔ Have I eliminated any patchwork quotations and mosaic paraphrases?

_____ ✔ Did I set aside my notes when I began writing my essay?

_____ ✔ Are all the words in my essay taken directly from my sources used inside quotation marks?

_____ ✔ Have I checked that quotations I have used are exact?

_____ ✔ Have I used ellipses and brackets when making changes in quotations?

_____ ✔ Do all quotations in my essay have appropriate citations?

_____ ✔ Are all the quotations used in my essay truly necessary?

_____ ✔ Are the arguments made in my essay my own?

_____ ✔ Have I acknowledged the ideas borrowed from others?

_____ ✔ Is the sentence structure of the essay my own?

_____ ✔ Are signal phrases used appropriately and sparingly in my essay?

THINKING ABOUT HISTORY

■ ■ ■

After studying this chapter, you should be able to
- Ask a wide variety of appropriate historical questions.
- Avoid common fallacies and assumptions when studying the past.
- Use inferences when encountering fragmentary historical sources.
- Appreciate the value and limitations of statistical evidence.
- Adopt a systematic evaluation method for historical sources.

Writing history involves a special way of thinking because the past in all its complexity cannot be recaptured like an instant replay. Real life has no instant replay; history does not repeat itself. The stuff of history—human experience—moves ceaselessly, changing endlessly in a process so complicated that it is like a turning kaleidoscope that never makes the same pattern twice. Consequently, knowing history is only possible through the stories that are told about it, stories that are told by many people, supported by many different kinds of evidence, told in different ways in different times and in different places. Historical research and historical thinking always involve listening to a multitude of voices, mute perhaps on the page but speaking through human intellect as historians try to sort them all out and arrive at the story that is most plausible.

A consciousness of history begins with the knowledge that present and past are different. The writing of history flourished when people fully realized that times were changing, that the new was replacing the old, and that the stories of the old should be written down before they were lost. Very soon historians understood as well that to write history means to make an effort to tell the story of the past in language that makes sense to readers in the present, an effort that may distort the story. Yet it is necessary because the past has such power. Human beings want to know how things got this way. They yearn to understand origins and purposes, and essential parts of their own lives in the present are influenced by their understanding of the past.

Not long ago debate was raised anew about the origin of an explosion that sank the U.S. battleship *Maine* in Cuba's Havana Harbor on February 15, 1898. Shortly after the event, American newspaper reports stirred public opinion to believe that almost two hundred American sailors were lost when the *Maine* was sunk by a bomb planted against its hull by Spanish agents. Not long afterward, the United States declared war against Spain. American troops defeated the Spaniards in Cuba, Puerto Rico, the Philippines, and other territories, and the United States acquired an overseas empire for the first time. Now some evidence seems to suggest that a fire in a coal bunker in the ship itself ignited ammunition stored nearby, sinking the ship. Historical research into the origins of that now distant war serves to make many people cautious when the government tells citizens today that the nation must go to war because its honor or morals are in peril if it does not. Present and past work together to condition attitudes toward both of them.

What *really* happened? That is a fundamental question everyone would like to know about the past. But the problems of history resemble the problems of memory. What were you doing a year ago today? If you keep an appointment book, you can find in it the names of people you saw that day. But what did you say to each other? The journal does not tell you everything. Someone might say to you, "I remember when we sat on the beach at Pawley's Island, South Carolina, year before last in August and talked about Elvis Presley's death." "Oh," you may reply, "I thought that was three years ago in a café in Charleston." You may have recorded the conversation in your journal; or you may have forgotten to make an entry that day. So where did the conversation take place? You have sources to check your own memories, as do historians. But like your own sources, those that historians look to may not provide immediate answers to every puzzle.

The sources for history have been conditioned by when they were created and are also conditioned in the present by how they are read. Increasingly historians are concerned about people's perceptions of events. For example, legends of the saints told in the Middle Ages are filled with miraculous happenings. St. Denis was said to have been beheaded in Paris while preaching to the pagan Gauls. Legend has it he walked with his head in his hands to the site that later became the monastery of St. Denis outside the city, and he set his head down there to mark the place where he should be buried. The kings of France were later buried in the monastery church built on the site. A statue of the saint, holding his head in his hands, stands now on the front of Notre Dame Cathedral in Paris, a reconstruction of a statue torn down by mobs in the French Revolution.

Most of us don't believe that people walk about holding their severed heads in their hands, yet you can respect this tale as a charming legend, not literal truth. Did the people of medieval Paris believe the story of the miracle? In a supremely reasonable attitude toward the past, you may assume that the story of St. Denis was a good way for the bishops of Paris to emphasize the importance of their city and the truth of the orthodox Christian theology they professed. Paris achieved a sacred status because of the miracle. But who can tell? Maybe the medieval bishops *did* believe the story! And perhaps you may have to revise your nice, reasonable explanations for its origins.

The stories historians tell are about human beings living in particular times and places. Human motives are in every age complex, mysterious, and often absurd. Many people in every land do crazy and destructive things for what seems to be no reason, and scapegoats for national calamities or imagined enemies are summoned up by hysterical leaders to be blamed and to have horror inflicted upon them. "Rational" people cannot believe St. Denis walked across Paris carrying his severed head in his hands. But how could "rational" people also acquiesce in the systematic slaughter of their supposed enemies, as in Armenia at the beginning of the twentieth century or in Rwanda nearer its end?

All this is to say that history involves you in modes of thought common to daily life as well as in the effort to understand acts and ideas utterly foreign to your own. Without doubt, we understand best the people of the past when their words and deeds, framed by their own times, speak to us in some way about the challenges we face in the present. Reaching such an understanding requires that you never shy away from asking questions and especially questions that occur to you based on your own contemporary concerns and interests.

HISTORICAL QUESTIONING

As you ponder the past, and especially as you study and read about it, keep in mind these familiar questions—*who, what, when, where,* and *why?*—as your guide; try to answer them briefly as you read and consider any topic. These questions correspond to an almost universal way that literate people respond to information, and they have long been used by historians trying to understand past events. As they focus on something that happened, historians ask *who* the people involved were, *what* exactly happened, *when* it happened, *where*, and *why*. The answers often overlap. To explain *what* happened is sometimes to explain *why* it happened. And you can scarcely separate a *who* question from a *what* question, because to write about someone is to discuss what that person did.

The overlap of questions is the very reason they are so useful in research. A complex event is like an elaborate tapestry tightly woven of many different-colored threads. The threads are distinct, but they are hard to sort out. These questions help keep your eyes on this or that important thread so you can see how it contributes to the whole. They will help immeasurably in analyzing human actions. The emphasis you place on one question or another may determine the approach you take to writing an essay about a historical event. And thus the focus of your questioning may alter the puzzles you identify and the story you will tell. Remember, too, that there is not just one *who* question or one *what* question or one *why* question. There may be dozens. Ask as many of them as you can. Push your mind.

These research questions can frequently help you work through the malady referred to as writer's block. All writers experience this affliction at one time or another. You cannot get started writing, cannot go on, or cannot finish. But it is important to find a place to make a start, even if it is only a small step. Try starting out by writing each of the questions about your topic that first occur to you; don't worry if they seem to overlap. Then try writing various answers to each of them. Often you can give your mind a push by writing out almost anything that occurs to you. Even a nonsense poem, composed out of your frustrations, may help inspire you to further writing. Certainly, writing stimulates the mind; we cannot emphasize that point enough. Almost any process that makes you write about your topic will fill your mind with thoughts you could not have had if you had not started writing first. Sometimes the rigid discipline of spending ten minutes each day writing a journal entry about your efforts—even if they have not produced anything else that day—can start you on further writing sooner rather than postponing your efforts until later. Or perhaps you can enlist a friend in an electronic chat about your efforts at a regular time each day as another means to jump-start your writing. But above all, don't retreat from your questioning without making *some* effort to write down *something* about your questions and, if you can, what answers you have begun to find.

"Who" Questions

Many historical topics center on individuals. If your topic is one of these, you will want to begin with *who* questions. Who was Pearl Buck? Whom did she write about? Who loved her work? Who were some of her critics? Who was influential in interpreting her work? As you ask such questions while reading your sources, keep a record of them and jot down the answers—or note that you don't know the answers. You should also recognize a multitude of other questions that occur as you do this. Where did she live in China? What did her missionary experience there contribute to her view of that country? What did she do to influence American attitudes toward China? Why did she win the Nobel Prize? When was the prize given to her? What did literary critics say about her work? What did her fans say about her? What do people say about her work now? When did the attitude about her work begin to change? Why did it change?

As you ask—and attempt to answer—these additional questions, your thought evolves. You begin to see relations between some of your questions. For example, you may push yourself to ask a dozen or more *where* questions or a multitude of *why* questions. And you may begin to read some of your sources differently. For example, you likely know that American public opinion was shocked when the Communists under Mao Zedong took over the Chinese mainland in 1949. Many politicians, including Senator Joseph McCarthy of Wisconsin, claimed that the United States had "lost" China for democracy because the U.S. Department of State was infested with Communist agents. Did Pearl Buck's idealistic books about China, especially her classic *The Good Earth*, help create an unreal impression of the situation there? Questions such as these can lead you to read—or perhaps reread—Buck's books, reviews of her work written in her own time, and articles written about her since. From them you can find your way to a good essay. And your initial *who* questions will have opened the door to your essay even though you will not write about all the answers you discovered.

"What" Questions

What questions, of course, have their basis in the fundamental problem for historical understanding: What happened? But as you probe further, asking *what* questions may involve weeding out legends and misunderstandings to see what really happened. A frequent question that will come to mind as you read your sources is, "What does this mean?" Often you will be trying to see what people in the past meant by the words they used. These meanings can confuse us because they often change. "What has changed in the understanding of this?" will also become an important question.

In the nineteenth century the word *liberal* was used to describe businessmen who wanted to make a place for themselves in a country ruled by an aristocracy with its power based on land. The liberals were capitalists who thought government ought to keep its hands off business. Most liberals believed that the economy ran by implacable laws of supply and demand and that any effort to help working people interfered with those laws and was bound to lead to catastrophe. In the twentieth century, the word *liberal* was used by Americans to describe those who wanted government to hold the balance of power between the strong and the weak, the rich and the poor. At the beginning of the twenty-first century, neither major American political party wants to use the word because it implies spending by the government for programs to help the poor and the weak, and consequent taxes to support that spending. In some political rhetoric the word *liberal* has become a special category for scorn.

Certainly relationships exist between the use of the word in these different ways. Liberals in both the nineteenth and twentieth centuries advocated "liberty," the root word of *liberal*. Nineteenth-century liberals wanted to create liberty for the business classes who suffered under customs that gave political power to landed aristocrats. Twentieth-century liberals tried to create more liberty for the poor, including the liberty to have a public school education with its recognition of talent and opportunities for advancement. What changed in American life to account for the difference in the concept of liberty? And what brought about the shift in attitudes toward the words *liberal* and *liberalism*?

When you use such broad terms in your writing, you must define what you mean by them. Be on guard against reading today's definition into yesterday's words. Don't rely only on easily available dictionary definitions, such as you might quickly find online. Be sure to look for the origins of words and their etymologies, including examples of how they have been used over time. Words are defined by their historical context in time and place, and you must be sure to understand what they originally meant, how that meaning has changed, as well as their usual meanings today.

In answering *what* questions, historians sometimes try to distinguish between the unique qualities in events and the qualities that seem to have ongoing relevance. For example, What qualities helped some large states endure for long periods of time? What qualities have seemed to doom others to fall? The questions are fascinating, but the answers are uncertain. One historian may see a pattern of repetition; another may see, in the same events, circumstances unique to a specific time and place. Some Greek and Roman historians believed that history involved cycles of repetition and that to know the past allowed people to predict the future. Few modern historians would make such claims. Some broad patterns do seem to repeat themselves. Empires, countries, and cultures rise and fall. To some scholars, these repetitions make it seem that all history is locked into invariable cycles. Viewing history in this way, though, suggests a treadmill on which human beings toil endlessly without getting anywhere. And it can limit the historian's capacity to discover what really happened.

"When" Questions

Sometimes you know exactly when something happened: the moment the first Japanese bombs fell on Pearl Harbor, the moment Franklin Roosevelt died, and exactly when the Confederate charge reached its high-water mark on the third day of the battle of Gettysburg. Of course this certainty is born of our acceptance of a common system of measuring time. Historians know this has not always been the case, and to some extent is not the case today. The Islamic method of reckoning time, for example, is based on different initial assumptions—the *hijrah* (or "flight") of Mohammed from Mecca to Medina, rather than the birth of Jesus—and a different method—lunar rather than solar—of calculating the passage of days. The history of calendars is itself a fascinating subject of historical study. Nonetheless, to avoid confusion historians generally accept the Western, or Gregorian, method of time calculation, and it has been a practical and realistic way to answer many *when* questions.

But asking when something happened in relation to something else can provide a fascinating topic of research. When did volcanic eruptions destroy the Minoan civilization on Crete? The question is related to the rise of power on the Greek mainland by states such as Athens and Sparta. When did Richard Nixon first learn that members of his White House staff were involved in the now infamous Watergate burglary of June 17, 1972? "When did you know?" became an important question put to Nixon and his aides in the subsequent investigations. That question has come to epitomize a skeptical approach to historical sources, one that is vital to historical writing. You would do well to adopt such a sense of skepticism in your own research and use it as you try to answer all these key questions about your topic.

"Where" Questions

Questions about where things happened can often be absorbing. No one knows exactly the location of the Rubicon River. Julius Caesar crossed it with his army in violation of a law of the Roman Republic that forbade the army to approach near the capital. But wherever it was, it has another name today. The Rubicon was in northern Italy and formed the border between the Roman province known as Cisalpine Gaul and the Roman Republic itself. But which modern Italian river was then called the Rubicon is a matter of dispute. However, deciding where the Rubicon was might help historians understand how much warning the Roman Senate had when Caesar moved with his troops on the capital.

Where questions involve geography, and you should think about geography when you write. Geography may not yield anything special for your work, but if you ask the right questions, geography may open a door in your mind onto a hitherto unimagined landscape of events and explanation. The Annales school of historical study in France made geography one of its fundamental concerns, asking questions such as how long it took to travel from one place to another in Europe, where the major trade routes were, where different crops were grown, and what cities had the closest relations to one another. For historians, good topographical maps showing roads, rivers, mountains, passes, coasts, and locations of towns have long been an indispensable resource. Modern online cartographic resources, such as Google Maps, may also help you ask better questions about your sources. But keep in mind that maps and geographic features do change over time, just like the meanings of the words used to describe them.

"Why" Questions

Sometimes you know what happened. But basic curiosity should lead you to ask *why* it happened. Why did it have the influence it did? These questions—essentially about cause and effect—create an eternal fascination. But cause and effect are like unruly twins. In historical study they are inseparable, yet it is often difficult to see just how they relate to each other. You might call the precipitating, or triggering, cause that which sets events in motion. The background causes are those that build up and create the context within which the precipitating cause works. Precipitating causes are often dramatic and fairly clear. Background causes are more difficult to sort out and often ambiguous.

The precipitating cause of the American Civil War was the bombardment and capture of Fort Sumter by the forces of South Carolina on April 12, 1861. No one would claim that the incident in Charleston Harbor all by itself caused the Civil War. Behind the events of that Friday morning were many complex differences between North and South. These were background causes of the war, and historians ever since have been trying to sort them all out to tell a sensible and precise story to explain why America's bloodiest war came.

Background causes offer rich possibilities for writing about the *why* of history. They allow writers opportunities for research, analysis, inference, and even conjecture. But precipitating or triggering causes can be worthwhile subjects in themselves. Exactly what happened at Fort Sumter on that April day in 1861? Why were passions so aroused on that particular day in that particular year? The *what* question and the *why* question come together—as they often do.

Good historical writing considers how many different but related influences work on what happens and sees things in context—often a large context of people and events. Nineteenth-century historians thought that if they understood the leaders, they knew everything needed to know about why historical events happened as they did. But thinking in context means you try to sort out and weigh the relative importance of various causes when you consider any important happening. As a result, more historians are now asking questions such as, Why did a rebellion of Indian soldiers in the service of the East India Company in 1857 in Bengal lead to massacres of British settlers all over India? Why were the British able to persuade other Indians to unite with them in committing horrifying atrocities to put down the rebellion? Such questions lead to investigations into the lives of people, often scarcely literate, who have left few written records behind. Since it is hard to resurrect the life of the masses, the problem of answering the *why* questions of history becomes complex, sometimes uncertain, yet very fascinating.

Some *why* questions may seem to have been answered more definitively. Yet an inquiring historian may reexamine the original puzzle and find another possible answer that changes or perhaps even contradicts accepted wisdom. Realizing the potential of this process—known appropriately as *revisionism*—should be motivation enough for caution in accepting uncritically what may seem to be settled historical truth. Such skepticism is an essential part of writing history. Asking questions that may have been overlooked, thinking about accepted answers in new ways, carefully reexamining the evidence, and discovering previously unexamined sources may all turn up new possibilities for retelling a story about the past. Yet this process does require care to ensure that you avoid the many common fallacies that often creep into historical writing.

HISTORICAL FALLACIES

"A fallacy is not merely an error itself," historian David Hackett Fischer observed a number of years ago, "but a way of falling into error. It consists in false reasoning, often from true factual premises, so that false conclusions are generated."[1] In his book on the subject, Professor Fischer suggested quite a number of specific fallacies—and offered examples of each from historical writing. For several years after his book appeared, historians scanned its pages hoping not to find their names included! For aspiring historians, though, a more fruitful approach is simply to keep a few of the common errors in mind so that you might avoid them in your writing.

You may be familiar with one common fallacy often associated with the term *straw man*. People set up straw men when they argue against positions their opponents have not taken or when, without evidence, they attribute bad motives to opponents. In a twenty-first century era when any-one with an opinion can acquire a soapbox from which to proclaim the most outrageous views, claiming an intellectual victory by arguing against ideas never espoused by an adversary is both common and unfair. Such an argument is simply beside the point. Worse, an opponent might advance an *ad hominem* argument, contending that an opponent is unworthy—based on some particular personal characteristic—to be believed. This fallacy, of course, is based on attacking the person making the argument rather than on the logic or evidence supporting it. Avoid the temptation. Be fair to opposing views, describe them accurately, and criticize them on their merits.

And you should also eschew the bandwagon fallacy, the easy assump-tion that because many historians agree on an issue, they must be right. Consensus by experts is not to be scorned. But experts can also be prone to prejudices or succumb to a desire not to be alone in their opinions. The democratic desire to seek a majority opinion is not always the best way to arrive at historical conclusions. Great historical work has been done by

---

[1]David Hackett Fischer, *Historians' Fallacies: Toward a Logic of Historical Thought* (New York: Harper and Row, 1970), xvii.

people who went doggedly in pursuit of evidence against the influence of a historical consensus. But be sure you have the evidence when you attack a consensus!

Another error in thinking—the fallacy of the single cause—sometimes emerges out of the difficulties in finding answers to complex *why* questions. A particular possibility may seem to be especially attractive, but it is almost always a mistake to lay too much responsibility for any happening on only one cause. Do not be tempted to give easy and simple causes for complex and difficult problems. For example, do not argue that the Roman Empire fell only because Romans drank water from lead pipes or that the South lost the Civil War only because Lee was defeated at Gettysburg. These events were caused by complex influences, and you should take care to acknowledge those complexities.

By all means you also should avoid the fallacy that comes wearing an elaborate Latin name—*post hoc ergo propter hoc*, "after this; therefore because of this." It refers to the fallacy of believing that if something happens after something else, the first happening caused the second. A more subtle problem with this fallacy arises with events that are closely related, although one does not necessarily cause the other. The New York stock market crashed in October 1929. The Great Depression followed. But it is a mistake to say that the crash caused the Depression; both seem to have been caused by the same economic forces. When you confront this sort of relationship of events in writing essays, you must carefully think out the various threads of causation and avoid making things too simple.

In a similar fallacy of oversimplification, many nineteenth-century historians believed that history was the story of inevitable progress, culminating in a predictable conclusion, such as the triumph of the white races because of their supposed superiority over people of color throughout the world. They viewed this as a step forward, making the entire world better as a result. Other historians have seen history moving according to God's will: When people do good, they thrive; when they violate the laws of God, they decline and suffer. But on close investigation, the swirls and waves of the historical process don't appear to move in such easily predictable patterns.

Likewise, those who assume that learning about the past will allow them to avoid mistakes in the future easily fall victim to fallacious assumptions; they underestimate the continuous flow of the "new" into human events. New inventions, new ways of thinking, or new combinations of ideas can upset all predictions. Most modern historians understand the need to be cautious in suggesting what history can tell us of both the present and the future. For one thing, few historians continue to predict inevitable progress in human affairs. It is possible to know history well and still be startled by events. In recent decades thousands of historians young and old studied the history of the Soviet Union. The Central Intelligence Agency employed historians to help the U.S. government understand how to deal with the Soviet Union and predict what it might do. Yet not one of these scholars predicted anything like the sudden collapse and breakup of the great Soviet empire in 1989 and 1990.

A similar fallacy, assuming the unchanging nature of some human societies—sometimes described as *traditional*—suggests that they will resist any sudden changes. Thus some historians and other scholars who study the Middle East were caught completely off-guard in 2011 when country after country in the region was shaken by revolutionary movements. A new group of historians will no doubt look back at those events with revisionist perspectives and find evidence from the recent past that might well have suggested possibilities for change that most had not previously seen. But doing so will require a careful review of evidence with new assumptions and a willingness to ask different questions. You should not be afraid to do so in your own work, even while you are cautious in avoiding fallacies.

MAKING INFERENCES

We certainly want to encourage you to apply your mind to your evidence and also, in questioning sources of information, to use the ability of the mind to infer. Humans manage their daily lives by making inferences. If in the morning you see low, dark clouds piled in the sky, when you leave home, you take along an umbrella. Why? You have seen such clouds before, and they have often meant rain. You infer by calling on past experience to interpret a present event or situation. You cannot always be certain that what you infer is true. Sometimes black clouds blow away quickly, leaving the skies clear so that you lug around a useless umbrella and maybe a raincoat all day long. But without inference humans would have to reinvent the world every morning.

Historians always infer some answers to their questions. They strive to make sense of a document, of other evidence, or of inconsistencies between several sources. They try to decide exactly what is reliable and to understand why the evidence was created, when it might have been, where, and by whom. The aim of inference is coherence. Historians try to fit what they know into a plausible whole. For example, you would likely infer that there is something fishy about documents that use words not coined until long after the purported age of the document itself. Suppose you read this sentence in the diary of a pioneer woman who supposedly crossed the plains on her way to California in 1851: "We are having a very hard time, and I know that Americans who drive through Nebraska in years to come on Interstate 80 will scarcely imagine what we have endured." You would immediately infer that something is seriously wrong with the claims of this document!

In practice, historians face similar problems in dealing with all sorts of evidence. This is particularly true when the written documents are missing, not very helpful, or seem to be inconsistent, and there is little if any other direct evidence that might easily fill in the gaps. But that does not keep a good historian from asking questions, and making inferences, in trying to tell a true story about the past. For example, after reading accounts of Hernando de Soto's sixteenth-century journey through what is now the southeastern United States, Alfred W. Crosby was struck by the inconsistencies between those descriptions and the accounts of the first intended settlers two centuries later.

> In eastern and southern Arkansas and northeastern Louisiana, where De Soto found thirty towns and provinces, the French found only a handful of villages. Where De Soto had been able to stand on one temple mound and see several villages with their mounds and little else but fields of maize between, there was now wilderness....
>
> In the sixteenth century, De Soto's chroniclers saw no buffalo along their route from Florida to Tennessee and back to the coast, or if they did see those wonderful beasts, they did not mention them—which seems highly improbable. Archeological evidence and examination of Amerindian place names also indicate there were no buffalo along the De Soto route, nor between it and salt water. A century and a half later, when the French and English arrived, they found the shaggy animals in at least scattered herds from the mountains to the Gulf and even to the Atlantic. What had happened in the interim is easy to explain in the abstract: An econiche opened up, and the buffalo moved into it. Something had kept these animals out of the expanse of parklike clearings in the forest that periodic Amerindian use of fire and hoe had created. That something had declined or disappeared after 1540. That something was, in all likelihood, the Amerindians themselves, who naturally would have killed the buffalo for food and to protect their crops.

The cause of that decline and disappearance was probably epidemic disease. No other factor seems capable of having exterminated so many people over such a large part of North America.[2]

Crosby's questions led him to seek additional information—in this case from ecology and geography—and then arrive at an answer on the basis of probable inference. As Professor Robert C. Williams has recently observed, "historians tend to utilize whatever evidence is at hand," often "applying science to questions of historical interest" in efforts to resolve puzzles about the past.[3] Frequently similar to the forensic evidence used in legal proceedings, these sources are sometimes generated specifically for historical purposes. For example, forensic pathology (including odontological examination of teeth) and DNA typing offered important clues to the identification of Tsar Nicholas II, his family, and their servants whose hastily buried bodies were unearthed in the 1990s, some eighty years after their murders. And similar methods, also applied in the late 1990s, offered evidence identifying the remains of the boy-King Louis XVII, son of Marie Antoinette and Louis XVI. But comparable DNA testing done at about the same time offered no such clear evidence on the matter of Thomas Jefferson and Sally Hemmings, only suggesting that Jefferson might have been the father of a child born to his slave.

Historians use other types of scientific evidence to reexamine some of their documentary sources as well. In some cases, chemical analysis has proved critical, not least for art historians seeking to establish the authenticity of paintings; the chemical composition of paints is often crucial in identifying modern forgeries purported to be the work of long-dead artists. Similar techniques applied in the late twentieth century to other forgeries, such as the so-called Vinland Map and the sensational lost diaries of Adolph Hitler, revealed both to be not quite clever enough forgeries. Despite the claims of noted historians that both offered important new sources about the past, both were shown by chemical analysis to have been created with either paper or ink which was not available at the time they were supposedly created.

---

[2]Alfred W. Crosby, *Ecological Imperialism: The Biological Expansion of Europe, 900–1900* (Cambridge, UK: Cambridge University Press, 1986), 212–213. We have eliminated Crosby's citation of the considerable evidence he consulted in reaching his conclusions.

[3]Robert C. Williams, *The Forensic Historian: Using Science to Reexamine the Past* (Armonk, NY: M. E. Sharpe, 2013), 3. Professor Williams offers narratives about a number of specific examples we discuss here.

Although you may not have such scientific studies available to test your sources directly, these examples should offer a caution as you seek to solve any historical puzzle: Look to all manner of sources in your efforts. As have many historians in recent years, you may find that the works of social scientists and even other humanities scholars offer intriguing possibilities. The theoretical and methodological approaches used by anthropologists, psychologists, sociologists, and political scientists to study groups of people in the present can also offer analytical frameworks for the study of people in the past. You might also follow the lead of historians who acknowledge that their source materials conform to sets of rules determined by the genre of those sources themselves. For example, a diplomat writes a letter, and his or her reader expects a certain formula of information presented in a certain style of language. These and other methodological innovations, derived primarily from literary scholars, have had a profound influence on the ways that historians approach the past; you might consider employing similar techniques in your essays. As did Professor Crosby in answering questions he had about the accounts of travelers and settlers in the southeastern United States, you may find sources related to your subject—or appropriate methods of analysis—that you can draw upon to infer conclusions to the historical questions you pose.

Quantitative Data and History

Even some sources, which on their surface seem to offer uncontroverted certainty, often require the historian to reach conclusions by inference. This is certainly true in the use of statistics, which has increasingly become a major source for writing history. Modern governments keep statistics with nearly religious passion, and other agencies, such as various polling organizations, collect statistics with the same avid compulsion. To some students of history, statistics seem tedious; to others they are exciting and open new windows to the past. But statistics require interpretation. "Like all data," warns Priya Joshi, a historian of British India, "statistics ought to be regarded as approximations at best, only as good as the tools to retrieve and manipulate them, and therefore only provisional until different or better statistics—or different or better methods of historical inquiry—emerge."[4] What historians infer from statistical data may tell a great deal, but if they infer badly, they can make serious errors.

---

[4]Priya Joshi, "Quantitative Method, Literary History," *Book History* 5 (2002): 273.

One of the more controversial historical studies based on statistics was *Time on the Cross: The Economics of American Negro Slavery* by Robert Fogel and Stanley Engerman, an effort to see the face of slavery by looking at statistics from slave days before the Civil War. This method, known since the mid-twentieth century as *cliometrics*—the study of human history primarily from the analysis of statistical, and especially economic, data—was given extraordinary prominence after the publication of *Time on the Cross*.[5] The book generated considerable discussion in scholarly circles, including much criticism. Many historians agreed with Thomas Haskell that it was almost hopelessly "shrouded in controversy."[6] The resulting skepticism did little to encourage a new generation of historians to take up quantitative methodologies.

More recently other scholars, including some historians, have reinvigorated the study of the past with new efforts to analyze quantitative data. *Why the West Rules—For Now* by historian Ian Morris uses mathematical models drawn from a vast storehouse of data to make conclusions about many societies over a broad expanse of time.[7] Other scholars, not all of them historians, have made similar efforts to create predictive equations based on creating databases of widely varied information from all parts of the world. These new approaches, now termed *cliodynamics* by the ecologist and evolutionary biologist Peter Turchin,[8] are based on an assumption that the cultural dynamics of many different societies are essentially similar. The resulting "big picture history" is much less specific than Fogel and Engerman's earlier efforts and much more akin to a science such as meteorology, content with predictive generalities and accepting of the contingencies—and uncertainties—in human behavior which have been

---

[5]Robert William Fogel and Stanley L. Engerman, *Time on the Cross: The Economics of American Negro Slavery* (Boston: Little, Brown and Company, 1974), 2 vols. The authors described the first as "the primary volume" of their work, containing a general discussion of the issues and their conclusions; volume two was reserved for evidence and detailed "technological, methodological, and theoretical bases" of the study; vol. 1, p. v.

[6]Thomas L. Haskell, "The True & Tragical History of 'Time on the Cross,'" *The New York Review of Books*, 22, no. 15 (October 2, 1975), p. 9, available at http://www.nybooks.com/articles/9075.

[7]Ian Morris, *Why the West Rules—For Now* (New York: Farrar, Straus and Giroux, 2010).

[8]See Peter Turchin, *Historical Dynamics: Why States Rise and Fall* (Princeton, NJ: Princeton University Press, 2003).

the stock and trade of historians for many years. This latest bent in quantitative history nonetheless does suggest that counting and measuring the past, even if not always as precise as some historians would wish, may help uncover a historical "truth that would not otherwise be evident."[9]

The task is easier because statistical information is now often available in precise, accessible, and usable forms, although sometimes the quantity of statistical information available may seem daunting. But the task is harder since you might easily feel overwhelmed by a project that can involve seemingly endless tables of numbers, charts, and graphs. The interpretation of such statistical data requires a high level of skill, and this can make the task even harder than it seems at first. Statistics as a discipline is substantial and complex, involving a rigorous introduction to the methods of interpreting the numbers so that they make sense. Even with such instruction, errors in interpretation are not uncommon. Numbers may provide a comforting appearance of exactitude, but the appearance may not match the reality.

Certainly, some questions are beyond the power of statistics to measure. Many critics of quantitative methods in writing history protest that its practitioners claim to know more about the past than they really do. Nothing takes the place, say the critics, of understanding history through the lively words of those who participated in it. To these more humanistically inclined historians, statistics are skeletons without muscle and breath. Quantitative historians reply that the humanistic historians often argue about the same old things and that statistics can indeed help unlock some historical puzzles. Thus, our advice is the same as that offered more than four decades ago by David Hackett Fischer: "Every historian should count everything he can, by the best available statistical method."[10]

Doing so requires that you understand the limits of statistical analysis and operate within those limits. If you write an essay based on quantitative research, be sure that you have enough data and that you know enough about interpreting statistics to avoid obvious errors. Learn the correct terminology for statistical analysis. (For example, you must know the difference between the *median* and the *average*, the significance of the *bell curve*, and you must have some idea of how a *random sample* is collected.) And be cautious in the inferences you draw from your evidence. Even if you have some knowledge of basic statistics, be sure you understand how such

---

[9]Joshi, 264.
[10]Fischer, 90.

methods are used in historical writing.[11] Ask your history instructors for advice or, with their guidance, you might also turn to other faculty at your university or college who teach statistics in one form or another and who understand the pitfalls of statistical research. You may be pleasantly surprised at the interest your queries generate.

In using statistical data, as with using any other evidence, when you make an inference important to your study of the sources, you become an active questioner. Remember the caution voiced by Professor Akinumi Ogundrian, director of the Upper Osun Archaeological and Historical Project on the history of the Oyo Empire: "History is not determined by the nature of the sources, but rather by the nature of the questions asked about the human condition."[12] Always read and analyze information about the past actively by asking questions, identifying puzzles, trying to fill in the gaps you may find, and making inferences as you do so. In the process, of course, you must also assess the value of what you read in helping tell the story about the past you want to write.

EVALUATING MATERIALS

This evaluation process is, of course, essential to historical writing. All historians, in one way or another, engage in making assessments of the materials they use in crafting their histories. These practices constitute the "critical method" of history, a key part of historians' special way of thinking, and encourage a healthy historical skepticism, so vital in evaluating historical sources of all kinds. At one time the evaluation process was primarily an effort to determine if historical documents were, in fact, genuine, that they were what they purported to be. A famous example involves a medieval document known as the Donation of Constantine.

According to the document, in the fourth century the Emperor Constantine was cured of leprosy by a pope, and in gratitude he moved from Rome to Constantinople, writing out this document giving political control of Western Europe to the pope and his successors. Several centuries

---

[11]As a starting point, we recommend Charles H. Feinstein and Mark Thomas, *Making History Count: A Primer in Quantitative Methods for Historians* (New York: Cambridge University Press, 2002).

[12]Akinwumi Ogundiran, "The End of Prehistory? An Africanist Comment," *American Historical Review* 118 (June 2013): 793.

later an Italian named Lorenzo Valla began to ask some questions about the Donation. Why did none of the people around Constantine who wrote about him and his reign mention his attack of leprosy or the Donation? Why did the document use words that were not coined until centuries later? Why was it not quoted by anyone until about the ninth century? Why did it make many historical errors? Valla inferred the work could not be about an actual historical event and that it could not have been written in the time of Constantine. Therefore, he concluded that the work was a forgery. Although his judgment wasn't immediately accepted by the papacy, his analysis has come to be been widely accepted by historians.

But the record of counterfeit historical documents is not limited to those created centuries ago. There have been a number of celebrated examples in more recent years of primary sources that were not what they seemed to be. Some, such as the Vinland Map and the Hitler diaries, have been exposed by scientific evidence. While it's unlikely you will have to make any such judgments about the authenticity of the primary sources that you use in writing your history papers, such experiences should suggest that you would be well served by a healthy historical skepticism. Perhaps if your sources were found in a discarded trunk or an abandoned attic, you will need to make an effort to determine if they are authentic. But many of the primary sources you are likely to employ will be found in published collections. You may reasonably expect the editors will have undertaken a careful examination of the documents prior to their publication. You may actually find other, unpublished primary sources in nearby archives or libraries, where the custodians of the original documents will have made such determinations.

Of course more and more sources about the past are becoming available on a variety of Web sites all the time. Some of these are associated with archives, libraries, and other reputable organizations, ones whose officials are likely to have made preliminary judgments, at least about the authenticity of sources presented. But obviously you should not be uncritically accepting of every Web site offering historical documents to researchers. You should always consider questions such as these: Who created and/or maintains the Web site? What organization, if any, sponsors this work? Does anyone responsible have particular interests in the content? If there appear to be no sponsors, is this the work of a single enthusiast? Certainly, individuals may create such Web sites for many scholarly or nonpartisan purposes. You may need to use the historian's skill of inference to answer some of these questions, at least in part. But if you are unable to locate any information about the sponsor or creator of a

Web page, that should give you pause. Remember the high value historians place on skepticism in evaluation of their sources!

In this spirit we also caution against an uncritical acceptance of any historical documents, including photographs, that you might find on the Internet. Sadly, the creators of some Web sites have been known to alter even well-known historic documents (perhaps most frequently by omitting select portions of text) in an effort to use the altered versions in support of a particular cause. And digital technologies have made adjustments in photographs and other images far easier than even in Stalin's day, when government officials of the Soviet Union disappeared from official photos of the national leadership after one purge or another. You will need to be vigilant as you look for primary sources. Keep foremost in your mind the skepticism of Lorenzo Valla as he read and reread the Donation of Constantine!

Such critical explorations of a Web site may not be nearly as tedious as they may first seem. You might find a gem of information tucked away in an unexpected place. We have experienced such serendipity more than once! And in any case, by taking a systematic approach to exploring a Web site, you will be engaging in the time-honored application of the historian's critical method. But remember you will still need to retain the same sense of skepticism as you apply to primary sources when it comes to the secondary sources, which will also be important for writing your essays. In doing so you can use the historian's questions—*who, what, when, where,* and *why*—along with the answers you find and the careful inferences you make, to help establish first if your sources are **plausible** and **trustworthy**, and then if they are **accurate** and can be **corroborated**. Those four standards of evaluation will serve you well as you read, and ask questions about, a wide variety of sources, including those you find on the Internet and in other electronic media. No matter where you find your sources, *you* must assume the role of primary evaluator of the information you find. Your readers, and especially your instructors, will expect you to do so carefully.

Certainly the commonsense test is one of the best you have at your disposal to begin your evaluations. Historians do have to trust their own insights. They need to make reasonable judgments based on their own sense of what is possible. So, first ask yourself: Is what I have found **plausible**? If what you are reading suggests that the Egyptian pyramids or the great stone statues on Easter Island were created by alien visitors from outer space, you have good reason to doubt them. The more fantastic the information and explanations you are offered seem to be, the more likely they will be simply fantasy. One application of this common sense rule is the philosophical and scientific principle known as *Ockham's razor*, after the ideas of the fourteenth-century English philosopher William of Ockham. Simply put, the concept suggests that simpler explanations are usually to be preferred over complex ones, especially when known information can be used to reach those simpler conclusions.

Yet even applying your mind in this way to determine if your source is plausible, what is it about a Web site (or any other source) that inspires you to see it as **trustworthy**? Can you detect any signs of bias, with any indication of partiality in one direction or another? Read carefully to see if there are lots of categorical assertions. Claims of *completely*, *never*, or *always*— as opposed to, say, *nearly*, *seldom*, or *usually*—can also be indicators that the authors may not have explored all the ramifications of the topic or, even worse, wish to convince you of a predetermined point of view. Also look for the qualities of impartiality and balance in the writing. Has the author (or authors) taken other opinions into account? Were those doing the reporting in a position to know what they reported? For example, were American veterans of the Korean War who reported Korean civilians were indiscriminately shot by U.S. soldiers actually serving in military units present at No Gun Re, where other Korean civilians claimed the attacks took place? Perhaps some of them served as medical corpsmen and treated the wounded. That could make their statements more trustworthy in your eyes.

Next, you will want to think about the **accuracy** of the information you have found. Although some historical information is almost timeless, you may make a start in thinking about accuracy by examining when a book or article was written or when a Web site was created and how recently it may have been updated. You can also look for other indicators of accuracy. Do the details match what is known and what can reasonably be inferred? In many British colonial territories, annual census figures remained the same year after year with no variation. District colonial administrators, it seems, did little more than make estimates and repeat the same details when new figures were required a year later, disregarding the improbability that births and deaths would exactly balance year after year. While few supervising officials in the British Colonial Office questioned such reporting, no historian would today consider such statistics to be an accurate reflection of a region's actual population.

Finally, as you would for any source, you should look for **corroboration** in other sources, not just on the Web but also in reference works and other—often printed—sources. While it is not necessary to reject information that you may not be able to affirm through other sources, you will certainly need to treat it more cautiously in what you write. Good historians try to do this, just as *Washington Post* reporters Bob Woodward and Carl Bernstein always sought other sources to confirm the details their famous informant, Deep Throat, passed on to them concerning what has come to be known as the Watergate affair of the 1970s. Keep in mind, as did Woodward and Bernstein, that your corroborating sources must be independent of one another if you wish to have real confidence in what you write. This does not mean that a single source must always be rejected. But without corroboration, you must establish through other applications of this critical methodology that you have, indeed, found valuable information on which to base your essay.

While it is true that good historians do not implicitly trust every source of information, neither do they trust their own first impressions. Nor do they merely pose random questions regarding what they read, what they hear, or what they see. The exercise of the historian's critical method demands a much more systematic application of the injunctions to ask questions and make inferences. Only in doing so can you really claim to have evaluated that information you have collected and have written an essay presenting a story about the past that makes any claim to being true. Nothing is quite so destructive to historians' reputations as presenting conclusions that do more to prove their own gullibility, laziness, or unwillingness to ask questions than to provide real insight into the meaning of the past. You can make a start at avoiding such appearances by keeping in mind the following checklist as you begin researching and thinking about sources for a new writing project:

Writer's Checklist for Evaluation

_____ ✔ What questions do I need to ask about this information?

_____ ✔ Can I be certain the source of the information is genuine?

_____ ✔ Is the information truly *plausible*?

_____ ✔ Am I confident the source is *trustworthy*?

_____ ✔ What leads me to think the information is *accurate*?

_____ ✔ How might I be sure the information is *corroborated*?

PREPARING FOR WRITING

■ ■ ■

After studying this chapter, you should be able to
- Focus your essays clearly on a specific topic.
- Develop strategies for initial research inquiries.
- Seek out key secondary sources on your topic.
- Identify appropriate primary sources.
- Begin writing before finishing your research.

All writing is hard work if it is done well, and writing history has some special problems. It is sometimes easy to assume that simply being familiar with life—or some particular aspect of human interactions—is sufficient. George F. Kennan, the American diplomat and historian, confessed to making this assumption when he accepted the 1957 National Book Award for his *Russia Leaves the War*:

> I am afraid that I took up the historian's task somewhat casually, never doubting that it would be easier to tell about diplomacy than to conduct it—and not nearly so great a responsibility. But as this work gradually wrought its discipline upon me, I was both surprised and sobered to realize not only how difficult but also how important it was.[1]

Few people will be as honored for writing history as Kennan, but you can learn to do it successfully—and thereby learn to do other writing well, too. The problems of gathering evidence, analyzing it, organizing it, and presenting it in a readable form are part of many writing tasks in the world of business, government, and the professions—including law, engineering,

---

[1]Quoted in *The National Book Award: Writers on Their Craft and Their World* (New York: Book-of-the-Month Club, 1990), 18.

and others. So you should expect to use your skills developed in writing history essays in whatever your future career may be.

All writers use some sort of process—a series of steps that lead them from discovering and refining a subject to writing a final draft. Different writers work according to different rituals. The two of us developed somewhat different ways of approaching our own writing. And we certainly recognize that within our lifetimes, the ways historians work—and write—have changed a great deal. The most significant of these changes, and the most obvious, is the widespread influence of computer technologies, their applications, and the explosion of ideas and knowledge shared on the Internet. One frequent analogy suggests the Internet is the most revolutionary mode of communication since the invention of radio; another asserts the impact of computers to alter the work of historians may even be greater than that of the printing press. To be sure, there are cynics, even among historians, who scoff at what they see as a naïve and all-too-prevalent assumption that everything useful is on the Internet. However, nearly all historians of our acquaintance do acknowledge the significant impact of the computer and the Internet on the study and writing of history. We feel certain you are among that number!

However, if computers have contributed anything new to the nature of history, such change "does not *fundamentally* affect the production of history," as the noted British historian, Professor Arthur Marwick, observed.[2] Thoughtful questioning, conscientious research, diligent evaluation, and careful editing all remain essential to historical writing despite the many ways electronic technologies affect each of these processes. "Writing is not simply a medium," we agree with Professor Jeff Jeske of Guilford College; "it is a tool of exploration, a voyage of discovery, one that leads not only to new ideas but clearer ideas."[3] Electronic technologies are a boon to that journey, though it continues to require the skilled work of all students of history to reach a destination yielding the stories about the past, intended to be true, which are the hallmark of historical writing.

Eventually you will find your own way of doing things. In this and the next chapter, we will walk you through some common stages of the

---

[2]Arthur Marwick, *The New Nature of History: Knowledge, Evidence, Language* (Chicago: Lyceum Books, 2001), 146, emphasis in original.

[3]Jeff Jeske, "Why Write," *Guilford College Writing Manual,* http://library. guilford.edu/guilford-college-writing-manual/why-write/write-to-learn/, (n.d.), accessed 30 June 2013.

work writers of history must undertake on their way to creating essays or books. Perhaps because we are aware of the different approaches we have both used, our intent is not to prescribe a fixed process; rather, we hope to offer suggestions that you may incorporate into your own way of preparing for and then completing your essays. Should your instructor suggest that you proceed in defined stages, by all means heed the advice! You might then use the suggestions we offer here to supplement your efforts.

At the outset, though, we want to make clear this is seldom a linear process—one step following categorically after another—leading directly to a written product. One step may instead take you back to reexamine what you have previously done; only then will you be able to finish the task at hand. Even after you have gathered, analyzed, and organized your information, writing the complete essay will likely take you back to those steps as well. The following suggestions may help by showing you how others write, but in the end you must develop the writing process that suits you best.

FOCUSING ON A TOPIC

Most history essays begin with an assignment. In college courses your assignments will usually be outlined in the syllabus the instructor passes out at the beginning of the course or in the questions asked on essay examinations. You should always read each assignment with great care, looking for an indication of the kind of topic your instructor wants you to write about, the evidence she wants you to use, and the length the paper should be. Follow those instructions carefully. The topic may be general within the limits of the course: "You will write a ten-page paper on a topic agreed on by you and the instructor." Or the topic may be explicit: "Write a ten-page paper on the reasons for the appeal of Lenin's 'April Theses' in 1917 during the Russian Revolution." In some courses you might be required to write an essay with more of a historiographic focus: "Alfred Crosby, Daniel Headrick, and Edward Said have all written books about imperialism. Write a ten-page paper exploring the differences in their attitudes toward modern imperialism."

Many college courses may instead—or in addition—require that you write shorter essays, either on topics written outside of class or in essay examinations. Often these shorter essays are on quite specific topics, and you should read the assignments carefully to be certain you understand them; we have some additional advice concerning such essays, as well as exam essays, in Appendix C. But many assignments in history courses—even on essay tests and for short essays—are more general. For many students finding a topic in such circumstances is an ordeal. Professional historians frequently have the same problem, so don't be discouraged as you begin your search. The ability to find your own topic reflects both how well you know the material and how you think about it. Defining your own topic is good discipline. A liberal arts education—including education in history—should teach you to ask questions and ponder meanings in every text and topic you encounter in life. Asking questions, being skeptical of the answers, and then asking still more questions are essential parts of all historical writing you will do.

You should be curious about people, events, documents, or problems considered in your courses. This curiosity should cause you to pose some questions naturally, and especially about topics related in some way to what you are studying. For example, in one course you might study the Russian Revolution of 1917, in another the American obsession with the dangers of communism and the Soviet Union during the Cold War, while in a third you might consider the music of Sergey Prokofiev. In studying and reading about any of these subjects, your curiosity might well lead you to thinking about the half-century history of the Soviet Union and its collapse in just a matter of months, something unforeseen (if sometimes hoped for!) by very few responsible persons. That amazing event should stimulate multitudes of questions you might ask to satisfy your curiosity about how such a thing could happen. And any number of those questions could well lead to an excellent topic for a history essay.

As you read and attend class, you can help yourself by keeping notes in which you not only jot down what you learn, but also the questions that occur to you, including—and perhaps especially—those without obvious answers. Keep a systematic record of all these questions, perhaps in a separate section of your class notebook. Or you might even keep a small, separate notebook—or a special computer file—entirely for these ideas and questions; a collection of such questions will have lots of potential paper topics in it. And never be afraid to consider a well-worn topic. Why did the Confederate army under Robert E. Lee lose at Gettysburg? What qualities of Christianity made it attractive to people in the Roman Empire during the first three centuries after Christ? What was *humanism* in the Renaissance? At first glance you may think that everything has been said that can be said. Indeed, many things have been written on all these topics. But when you look at the sources, you may discover that you have an insight that is new or at least different in some way and worth exploring.

That possibility is especially good if you study a few primary source documents carefully and use them as windows to open onto the age or the event that produced them.

Sometimes you can find interesting topics in history by staying attuned to your own interests and experiences. If you are a religious person, you may naturally try to understand religious influences in the past. Do not use a history paper to convert someone to your own religious point of view. But religion is one of the most important continuing forces in world affairs, and it sometimes strikes us as odd that students do not think to apply their religious interest to exploring how religion has influenced historical events. The same is true of interests such as sports, food, fashion, and other elements of life. History is as open a field of study as your imagination allows. One of our students wondered how she might answer questions from her children about the bananas they frequently ate for breakfast. So she did some reading, thought about the problem, posed a number of questions, and the final result was an excellent history essay on how bananas became such a popular food in the United States although almost none are actually grown commercially here.

We must, however, repeat an important axiom: Yours must be an *informed* interest. You have to know something before you write anything about history. Do not write an opinionated essay merely off the top of your head; your argument needs to be more than a restatement of your preconceived ideas. Good historians read, ask questions of their reading, read again, and try to get things right. Theirs is a conversational approach to the past, as we discussed in Chapter 1. They try to think through their initial questions, examining the many facets of the problem and focusing on a narrower topic, one manageable within the limits of the essay they expect to write. You should do the same.

In our experience the most common flaw in student essays is that the topics are so broad that the essays have no focus; their writers have not tried to refine the topics and cannot therefore develop an original idea based on the evidence. You cannot write an interesting and original paper entitled "Woodrow Wilson" or "Mahatma Ghandi" or "Susan B. Anthony." In two thousand or even six thousand words, you can only do a summary of a person's life—-suitable perhaps for an encyclopedia but not for a thoughtful essay that tries to argue a special point. Similar difficulties would apply should you decide to write on "The Causes of World War II," or even "The Reasons for the Renaissance"; both topics are so broad as to defy any meaningful analysis in an essay of ten pages or so. You can use such ideas as a starting point, but delve deeper into them and focus on a limited issue with available primary sources or other evidence that you can study in-depth and write about within the assigned space.

Even if your instructor assigns a specific topic as the basis of your essay, it is almost always appropriate to limit, or at least focus, the topic further. Consider the topic we mentioned previously: "Alfred Crosby, Daniel Headrick, and Edward Said have all written books about imperialism. Write a ten-page paper exploring the differences in their attitudes toward modern imperialism." You will, of course, need to read the books of the three authors and determine the thesis each presents. Then you will need to compare the three views, analyzing how they are similar and different. These comparisons should lead you to a conclusion, and with it a specific argument (or thesis statement) for your essay "exploring the differences" in the theories about the causes and consequences of imperialism.

Whatever your writing assignment, or the general topic you first identify, there are usually ways to limit your topic either by narrowing its scope or adjusting your angle of vision. A broad topic such as imperialism, for example, might be reduced by focusing on the colonial ambitions of a single country. Even the scope of French imperialism could be further limited by considering French imperialism in the Caribbean, or even the island of Martinique alone. The geographic scope of your topic can frequently be reduced by also considering elements of time. You might consider limiting your consideration of imperialism to the period before—or after—the Napoleonic wars, for example. Or you might wish to consider the impact of twentieth-century developments—such as the League of Nations or the United Nations—on French imperialism in Martinique.

But in addition to limiting the scope of your topic, you might also consider changing your angle of vision. As we've previously noted, historians in this new century have successfully explored a much broader range of questions about the past. Years ago the usual concerns regarding colonialism were of grand politics or perhaps the details of colonial administration. You might also find occasional biographies of the key leaders. But with the changes taking place in the way historians observe the past, there are many more angles you might pursue to narrow your topic. You might ask questions not just about individuals, but also about specific groups of people. What were the effects of French imperial practice on the indigenous inhabitants of Martinique? Did French education policies in its Caribbean colonies increase the educational level of women as well as men? There are many other such puzzles that might well occur to you. In short, allow your curiosity to open new avenues of questioning as you consider your topic.

Surely you will find several ways you might further narrow that topic so that you can craft an interesting essay with a new argument.

In the process of making your essay more focused, however, you also need to keep in mind that your topic must be defined according to the sources available. In some cases your assignment will do this for you; on essay examinations, in particular, you are likely limited by the assigned materials you have read or heard about and discussed in class. But often you will need to determine what sources you might consult before completing your essay. Just as your interest in a topic needs to be an informed one, your approach to writing about that topic needs to be based on initial inquiries concerning what has been written and what sources are available. Your challenge in refining and narrowing your topic should simultaneously be one of expanding your quest for usable information. We encourage students to make these first searches as wide as possible, reminding them that almost always they will locate much more information than they can use in their essays.

MAKING INITIAL INQUIRIES

Indeed, the vast and still growing potential of the Internet and the World Wide Web may be the easiest means of finding out if what at first seem to be historical puzzles really are worthy of further questioning. You will be able quickly to find an astounding number of Web pages mentioning almost any topic. Always remember, however, that anybody with a World Wide Web connection can set up a Web page! Enthusiasts for this or that writer or painter or celebrity, both living and dead, and from anyone with a particular point of view they wish to promote, can create a Web page. Naturally enough, various fanaticisms abound in this virtually uncontrolled electronic environment. If you want to post a Web page and maintain that you were abducted by space aliens who introduced you to Abraham Lincoln in another galaxy, nothing can stop you. Given the variety of American society, you'll probably get a following who will tell you about their own conversations with Lincoln in outer space!

A popular twenty-first-century source for quick information is Wikipedia. Created in 2001, with more than four million entries by 2013, this seems an ideal place to find information about virtually any topic. Indeed, a recent report suggests it is among the seven or eight most popular sites on the Internet. Some reviews by respected observers have concluded that on many crucial scientific topics, the information available on Wikipedia is often more up to date than some print encyclopedias and contains fewer errors. Yet you should exercise an abundance of caution about relying too quickly on any Wikipedia article to answer your initial questions about historical topics.

A brief visit to the intriguing Wikipedia Vision site, created by László Kozma, will demonstrate the origins of our advice that you proceed with caution.[4] On the site you will see a world map displaying the location of individuals who make changes to many English-language Wikipedia entries almost as soon as they happen. Anyone with an axe to grind on a particular subject can alter information. Of course, any electronic vandalism can be corrected. Scores of volunteers work as diligently as possible to reduce the effects of malicious editing to Wikipedia entries, but at times it seems as if they are more like an understaffed militia trying valiantly to stop a serious crime wave! In any case you may never again be able to find that one piece of information that once seemed so crucial to your essay.

Despite problems such as these associated with open access to the Internet, you should not dismiss the Web as a tool for inquiry. Many Wikipedia entries have significant bibliographies which may be of great use in your research, and in any case what you find there may open your eyes to additional lines of inquiry. Other valuable and important resources are also available on the Web, and they are growing. To help you harness this potential, no doubt you will want to use one of the wide variety of available *search engines* to connect with Web sites containing some information on topics which interest you. The most popular, and some claim the most effective, is currently Google, at http://www.google.com, with a revamped Yahoo! search engine, at http://www.yahoo.com, and the newer Bing search engine, http://www.bing.com, not far behind. Each of them attempts to rank the relevance of the results concerning your search keywords based on a secret formula, or algorithm, which evaluates how many links each has to other relevant Web sites. This approach, some critics claim, creates a caste system in which some Web sites determine the popularity of others dealing with the same topics.

All search engines, however, are only as useful as the search terms you enter! Most have advanced search options, and we encourage you to use them. This will help you eliminate obviously unwanted information and narrow the results to those items most related to your interests.

---

[4]László Kozma, Wikipedia Vision (beta), http://www.lkozma.net/wpv (2008), accessed 01 July 2013; the FAQ link at the top of screen details operation of the site.

Draw on your first efforts to find further terms for new searches. Also consider using synonyms and phrases that explain the topic you are inquiring about. Don't make just a single effort, or become discouraged after even a second or third attempt. You will frequently need several attempts to find the great variety of resources available. Consider this just a part of the hard work involved in writing history essays.

When you review the initial results, remember that most search engines also prominently feature those sites whose operators pay to have their addresses advanced ahead of other search results. Sometimes these sponsored results are clearly identified, but not always. And search results may not be the same each time you make an effort. In fact, the operating parameters of most online search engines are frequently changing. This does not diminish the value of the search, but it should serve as a warning when you move beyond your initial explorations to more serious research on your topic.

As you continue your initial inquiries, also remember the advent of reliable electronic communications has made it possible for you to seek help from any number of historians and other scholars. Possibilities for discussion roar across the Internet every moment, including news groups, chat rooms, blogs, and instant messaging services. Some might be of help to you as you ponder the issues about which you may wish to write. Their informal nature makes them attractive electronic places in which to consider questions about your topic. This informality has an important place in encouraging the kinds of questioning that you must do as you start the writing process, and it may also offer excellent opportunities to begin writing about a potential topic.

Some of these—especially social media sites such as Twitter, Facebook, Pinterest, and others that will no doubt appear after this is written—can be comforting in their reach to like-minded people. This can be a major advantage for some purposes, such as organizing protests and calls to action. The use of such sites in shaping political events in the first few years of the twenty-first century has been remarkable, and some would say "historic." Professor Krista Sigler recently suggested that for contemporary historical research, "tweets" might be considered "a highly searchable cross between oral history and traditional memoir."[5] But such claims should not beguile you into thinking of social media as go-to avenues for research on

---

[5]Krista Sigler, "Teaching Twitter: The History of the Present," *Perspectives on History: The Newsmagazine of the American Historical Association* 49, no. 4 (April 2011): 37.

most topics. At least two characteristics of these forums mitigate against their usefulness. The first involves what some observers describe as their essential performance nature. Most of the messaging is calculated more to impress than to inform. The result, as many critics lament, is a second tendency, for the communication on these sites to become almost an echo chamber, with answers repeated over and over rather than being thoughtfully considered.

Perhaps of more interest to those seeking answers to historical questions, however, are somewhat more formal discussion lists comprised of people interested in a particular topic to which the list is dedicated. Some, however, remain free-for-all forums where anything sent to the list is immediately resent to all the e-mail boxes registered for the group. Others are presided over by one or more moderators or editors who ensure only messages germane to the list topic will be posted. Many such listservs in the latter group are of special interest to historians, especially those sponsored by the scholarly collective known as H-Net, Humanities and Social Sciences Online. You can find the directory of more than one hundred H-Net discussion networks at http://www.h-net.org where you can also access logs that archive previous messages. Although not all of them are strictly devoted to history, most do consider topics with broad historical dimensions. They range from H-World, devoted to many issues in World History, to H-Quilts, considering the history and making of quilts, to H-Tennessee, with discussions and information mostly about the history and geography of that state; there are many others focusing on a variety of topics.

All these H-Net discussion networks offer the opportunity to ask questions about many subjects—books and articles, puzzles in evidence, current problems—anything at all relating to the interests the group is intended to serve. Each has its own rules, including ways to join and ways to end your membership. We would offer one note of caution. A potential danger of belonging to several such groups is that your electronic mailbox may fill up quickly, and you might receive a great deal of information you don't want or need. When you join, however, you may be given an opportunity to set your options so that this problem is reduced, often by receiving daily digests of collected messages. Be sure to read the welcome message you first receive to discover how to do this. Such groups do form valuable scholarly communities, and you can tap into them in various ways not only to begin your own inquiries into a potential topic but also to eavesdrop on postings that may later aid you in your research. H-Net discussions are somewhat more formal than the freewheeling social media and blog sites, yet they remain informal ways to begin your questioning process and search for information.

Even as we encourage students to make full use of electronic possibilities, we have often been disappointed that they treat such efforts as the full extent of possible sources of information. By all means, you should also read articles in print encyclopedias and other reference materials to get a broad overview of your topic. If you look up the same subject in many different reference works, essential facts about your topic will be stamped in your memory. And don't forget that old reference books are valuable for providing widely held beliefs about topics when those books were published, and some—such as the eleventh edition of *Britannica*, published in 1911—are justly famous for the quality of their entries. Your library reference room will have standard, multivolume general encyclopedias and single-volume reference works such as *The New Columbia Encyclopedia* (one of our favorites). Many encyclopedias are also available in digital formats through electronic networks in your library and on the Internet, as is the *Britannica,* eleventh edition, at http://www.1911encyclopedia.org. Just as with Wikipedia, you may find this an interesting place to begin your inquiries.

Also look for reference materials that specifically address your field of inquiry. Not only broad fields of study such as art or music, but also historical specialties such as colonialism or even the history of peace and peacemaking are considered in valuable reference works. One we consult often is the seven-volume *New Dictionary of the History of Ideas* in which you may often find information about ideas you intend to discuss in your history essays. (The original five-volume *Dictionary of the History of Ideas*, published in the 1970s but now out of print, is available online at http://etext.virginia.edu/DicHist/dict.html.) Likewise, we often consult *Brewer's Dictionary of Phrase and Fable*, available in many editions since 1870 (the 1898 American edition is available online at http://www.bartleby.com/81), and the much more recent *Dictionary of Historical Allusions & Eponyms*, compiled by Dorothy Auchter, as a starting point for thinking and writing about all sorts of historical puzzles.

If you are considering a topic related to religion, you might consult *The New Catholic Encyclopedia* in fifteen volumes, which contains a treasury of information on religious figures and religious movements of all sorts. (The original *Catholic Encyclopedia*, published in 1915, is online at http://www.newadvent.org/cathen/.) *The New Standard Jewish Encyclopedia* provides a similar source for the history of the Jewish people and Judaism. (The earlier *Jewish Encyclopedia*, originally published between 1901 and 1906, is now available online at http://www.jewishencyclopedia.com.) And should your potential topic involve prominent individuals, you should consult one of the many biographical directories created for both broad and more narrow subjects of study. The *Dictionary of National Biography* is indispensable for any work on British history. The *Dictionary of American Biography* is inferior and sometimes disappointing, but one can find there interesting information about important Americans who may be subjects of historical research. Many libraries have old nineteenth- and twentieth-century biographical encyclopedias of local areas; these aren't to be scorned, although the articles are nearly always laudatory, and it seems as if the people—nearly all of them men—paid in some way to have their names included, perhaps by buying copies of the books.

Don't dismiss using reference works in foreign languages too quickly. Even if you don't read the language, you may locate illustrations, maps, or other useful materials. If you have had a year or two of study in the language, you may discover that you can read the articles far better than you suspect. That discovery may draw you into further use of the language, an advantage to any student of history and essential to advanced work in most historical fields. Some of the articles you find—as is true of many reference works in English—will have brief bibliographies at the end listing standard works where you can find more detailed information on a subject.

Among the most important reference resources for historians are bibliographies on a huge variety of topics, both broad and narrow, some compiled by scholars specifically as reference works and others included by historians in their books and articles. Often you will find numerous bibliographies in library reference collections, and you may frequently locate others using library catalogs by looking for or adding the subcategory "bibliography" to the subjects you are searching for. There are a number of valuable general bibliographies as well. Be sure, for example, you consult the widely available *American Historical Association Guide to Historical Literature*, now in its third edition, edited by Mary Beth Norton and Pamela Gerardi. These two large volumes are a rich mine of information about books and articles on every aspect of history throughout the world. You may also find some specialized bibliographic references on the World Wide Web. A few bibliographies are annotated. That is, the compiler offers a brief comment on the books, articles, and other materials cited. It is possible the writer may judge some sources too harshly, some too generously. But such a bibliography usually provides worthwhile information about the contents of books and articles. And the bibliographies and notes in the books you read have an added advantage: They usually reflect the best judgments of the authors concerning the most significant works on the topics.

It is up to you to seek out such resources for your initial inquiries and to ask for assistance when you need it. We affirm our advice in earlier editions of this book—that smart students and smart professors should learn to talk with reference librarians about sources of information. And those discussions should transcend matters of books and encyclopedias to encompass electronic search techniques and information retrieval, as well as the evaluation of sources. There are many reference works and research tools devoted to a wide variety of topics and many more are published each year. It is the job of reference librarians to be familiar with many of these; take advantage of their knowledge (and that of your instructors). Follow their suggestions about reference resources that may be available for your use. However, if you were to ask a reference librarian every single question that occurred to you about a potential topic, it is unlikely the results would be uniformly satisfactory. There is much you can—and *should*—do to find information before seeking help in your search.

IDENTIFYING KEY SOURCES

The more complete your initial inquiries into a potential topic are, the more likely those efforts will lead you toward key substantive sources which you can actually use to research the topic you finally settle on. Having used your initial inquiries to help refine that topic, you will now be in a position to make use of a variety of tools, many of them indexes to information, in building a potential list of both secondary and primary sources, both essential if you are to write a good historical essay. We mentioned in Chapter 1 the basic characteristics historians generally use to differentiate those two types of sources. Here we want to offer some further advice, particularly about how you might proceed in locating these substantive sources after you have finished your initial inquiries.

Secondary Sources

Secondary sources, created from an analysis of primary sources, will be an important part of the information you will use to write a history essay. Secondary sources are the work of historians, and others, who set out to explain the past based on what they have learned from examining materials created at, or otherwise connected to, the times being written about. You would do well to first turn to such sources as you collect information for your project. Many of these will be articles in scholarly journals or other periodicals dealing with historical topics. Some journals publish articles about particular facets of history—the Middle Ages, military affairs, science, art, women—or the history of particular parts of the world—France, Africa, the Middle East, Kentucky. Others, such as *The American Historical Review* and the *Journal of World History*, have a scope as wide as the discipline itself. Just an hour or two spent perusing such periodicals may well open your eyes to many issues that touch on your subject. And since the essays you write in a history course are more like journal articles than books, the journals will provide models of writing and thinking that you can emulate.

An essential tool you will need to master in order to tap into this expansive array of secondary sources is the variety of indexes which can help you locate articles in magazines and scholarly journals. Many of these are subscription services that are generally only available in libraries. You should establish which ones your college or university offers. Then seek help from reference librarians for assistance in accessing those that might be useful for research on the topic you are writing about.

Most of these have their origins in the venerable *Reader's Guide to Periodical Literature,* which has been regularly published since 1900. The new online version covers articles published since 1983, while *The Readers' Guide Retrospective: 1890–1982* provides information online on that earlier period. *The Reader's Guide* surveys only magazines intended for a general audience. Don't scorn this purpose. Although you will not find articles published in the specialized journals intended for professional historians, you may find interesting, well-written articles by important specialists when consulting *The Reader's Guide.*

Several *Info-Trac One File* electronic databases provide more extensive coverage, including both popular and academic periodicals, as well as some other similar information, such as transcriptions of National Public Radio programs. But this resource only deals with materials published since the 1980s. Another broadly inclusive database, which indexes not only journals but also newspapers and other important historical sources such as British Parliamentary Papers, is *ProQuest.* Since it brings together a number of previously separate search utilities, the depth of coverage varies depending on the information you are seeking.

In a few cases, these electronic databases may also permit you to locate the text of entire articles. A favorite of historians, which often produces quick results, is JSTOR, the Scholarly Journal Archive. You can search the full text of more than two hundred fifty specialized journals in history and others in related fields, covering the full run of issues usually up to about five years before the present for most titles. And you can receive electronically copies of individual articles you wish to read for your research. (These will be sent as portable document files, usually known as pdfs; to read them you will need to have the

Adobe Acrobat Reader installed on the computer, tablet, or even smartphone you are using for your research. This is available free at http://www.adobe.com.) As are many of the indexes, JSTOR is available through libraries that subscribe to its service; more than fifteen hundred U.S. institutions (mostly colleges and universities) currently do so, as well as nearly thirteen hundred others worldwide. Listings of subscribing institutions can be found at http://www.jstor.org. Without doubt, JSTOR is an especially valuable research resource, and you should inquire if it is available through your library.

Some libraries may also, or alternatively, subscribe to Project Muse, a service offering access to about three hundred academic journals, in a diverse array of fields. Its database is also fully searchable throughout the full text of all available articles. And if your library subscribes, you can receive electronic copies for your research of articles from journals selected by your institution. Project Muse emphasizes access to contemporary issues of journals, though for most of its holdings it does have some back issues available, at least to the date when a particular journal was first available through Project Muse. But for most journals the database does not include all the back issues, unlike JSTOR, which has extensive holdings of back issues; for example, issues of *The American Historical Review* in the JSTOR database go back to its first publication in the nineteenth century!

Many other electronic databases have thoughtful abstracts prepared by expert readers. Often using such abstracts can save you time, but you should be cautious in assuming they will always provide clear and complete indications of an article's content. Two such indexes are especially important for historians. Particularly strong for its coverage of world and European subjects, *Historical Abstracts* has appeared each year for many decades and in electronic formats since 1981. Its pages, disks, and now Web files contain thousands of abstracts of books and articles indexed according to author, subject, period, and place. You can browse the abstracts for materials related to almost any historical topic. *America: History and Life*, updated annually, includes article abstracts and citations focusing on American history, and also an index to book reviews. It goes back to 1964 and, like *Historical Abstracts*, is a fabulous resource. Both of these are subscription services but are widely available in most college and university libraries; you should consult with a reference librarian about how to access them in your library. It may be that you will need to peruse bound volumes for earlier years of some such indexes and perhaps for all the years of other indexes. Don't be put off by this eventuality, for ignoring such valuable resources will do little to enhance your essays; bypassing them can only keep you from finding potentially valuable articles.

Of course, articles will not be the only secondary sources you will need to locate. Make it a habit to look carefully at the resources of your university or college library, most especially the catalog of the library's holdings of books as well as other materials. Although there are a variety of systems libraries use to present their catalogs for research, most have similar features. Online catalogs have become the most common and usually allow you to search for materials by *author* and *title* as well as by *subject* or *keyword*. Keep in mind that for a library catalog, the subject usually refers to a uniform set of subject headings created by the Library of Congress. You will have to enter these *exactly* for a subject search to be successful. If you choose the *long* or *full* catalog record of a work you have already identified, you can find some appropriate subject headings for your topic. Easier still, you can search most library catalogs by *keyword*, usually a name or topic of particular interest to you. And most often you can also refine that search by either including or excluding other particular terms or specifying that a particular phrase should appear exactly as you have given it. Most catalogs have easy links to instructions guiding you in making such advanced searches. The results, however, will only be to materials that have been preselected for inclusion in your library.

In some libraries the books available may be extensive, but in others, they may not be nearly so voluminous. So don't limit your initial search for material to just what is easily at hand. One expansive resource that may be available in your college library is *WorldCat*, a worldwide union catalog of holdings in about nine thousand libraries associated with the Ohio-based Online Computer Library Center. Even if it is, you may wish to access it from your tablet or mobile smartphone by entering this URL—www.worldcat.org/m/—on your phone's Web browser or, alternatively, purchasing a *WorldCat* application program. Another resource readily available on the Internet is an integrated online catalog of almost twelve million bibliographic records from the Library of Congress; you can access it at http://catalog.loc.gov. You may also be able, either through your own institution's library or on the Internet, to find catalogs of other educational, public, or specialized libraries—you might also search some of them for information relevant to your topic. If you find materials in a nearby library, you may be able to look at them there or even, in some cases, borrow materials much as you would in your own college library.

If that is not possible, or all you have is a promising title which you want to peruse for your project, consider making an *interlibrary loan* request for an article or book that seems to be in the collections of another library. Internet connectivity has made this process much easier and more widely available, so you should certainly ask at your local library if it might be possible for you to make such a request. Don't be surprised if the result—for some books and especially for journal articles—is an electronic file to read in your library or on your own computer or other device. Or you may also have the option of an electronic book version of a title you need for research. While commercial publishers and booksellers are working hard to promote this option, the growing e-book collections may be available to you through your campus library or even using free access through Google Books (at http://books.google.com) or the World Public Library (at http://www.netlibrary.net/). An increasing number of such titles are also available for some portable electronic devices.

One alternative to reading every book that might be a potential source involves reading book reviews. A review may well tell you whether the book repeats old information, breaks new ground, contradicts received interpretations, and often whether the book is well written or almost impossible to understand. Some of the indexes and databases we have mentioned— including many that are available in electronic versions—can help you find book reviews. If it is available to you, also try *Book Review Digest*. It has indexes of published book reviews for nearly a century, and its online subscription version has reviews and summaries of books published since 1983. In this specialized resource, you can search for reviews by the names of book authors, usually in the years immediately after the book was first published. While the *Digest* includes some academic journals, it also includes more popular reviews for an intelligent reading public. But these sorts of book reviews may also contain valuable insights about your potential source.

While a growing variety of Web sites also offer increasingly more book reviews online, H-Net Reviews, which are found at http://www.h-net.org/ reviews, are particularly valuable, especially for books published in recent years. Most of the scholarly networks affiliated with H-Net: Humanities and Social Sciences Online commission book reviews, and literally thousands of those reviews are archived on this site. Perhaps more significant, the entire database can be searched using keyword terms or other parameters you select. This electronic review archive is an extraordinary research tool.

As you read book reviews, you will soon discover that occasionally reviews can be fiercely polemical, displaying historians at their worst. Of course some books deserve to be attacked because they ignore scholarly evidence or present a one-sided view of their subject. More often, uncivil reviews reveal pettiness and sometimes jealousy, and it is unfortunately often true that historians with radically new insights into a historical problem may be pummeled by old believers who think the truth was discovered long ago and is not subject to change. Still there is hardly any better way to be introduced to the historical profession than by reading lots and lots of book reviews. You should by all means read as many reviews of the same book—especially among your potential secondary sources—as you can, since different scholars will highlight different aspects of a book. You will often pick up information that you might otherwise miss and then be in a better position to evaluate the book as a source.

Increasingly there are other secondary sources besides books and articles that you may need to consider, and not merely those similar materials posted on Web sites. Some of these will almost certainly be in other than written form, including cinematic interpretations of subjects related to your topic. Historic events and characters have long been the subjects of films, both those meant to document what actually happened and those intended only to entertain by presenting versions of the past. With the increase in the number of television outlets, notably *The History Channel*, as well as the easy availability of compact disks and downloadable video files, these cinematic versions of the past have become a much more common source of historical information. Almost all of them are secondary sources since they represent the past as seen and interpreted by filmmakers. Even the best documentary films—such as those about American jazz music, baseball, and the Civil War created by Ken Burns—are not themselves primary sources, but clearly the creation of skilled storytellers and artisans working with primary sources to present an interpretation about events in the past.

Many feature films have historical themes or topics—some fairly recent examples we have seen include *Lincoln* and *The King's Speech*—are intended to be faithful representations of times past even though historians frequently criticize them for numerous inattentions to historical detail. In any case, films do provide a dramatic connection to the past, one which may especially satisfy our desires to visualize what we might otherwise know primarily from written texts. Moreover, they offer many people images that have a profound effect on how they read history essays. Thus, films on subjects related to your topic can, and often should, be among the sources you consult as you prepare to write an essay. But keep in mind you will need to evaluate them, not judging them on the format through which they reach you, but on the same critical basis as we have suggested for other sources.

You may also look for secondary sources in other popular media, such as newspapers and magazines. Occasionally both types of publications will feature the analysis of a particular subject, which will include, or may even primarily be, a consideration of the historical background of a particular topic. Perhaps because journalists ask similar questions, many of these articles can often be useful in your historical research. A few major newspapers, such as the *New York Times* and *The Times* of London, have cumulative indexes to subjects and authors appearing in their columns, and their issues are widely available in either or both microform and online versions. Some have searchable databases online, although often access may be limited to those who subscribe to the service. But once you have located—and evaluated—such stories, some may be very important to the essay you will write.

Primary Sources

Of course, newspapers may also contain primary sources. Since you want, if at all possible, to find primary sources about your topic as well, newspapers may be a good place to look. Accounts of direct observation of events by journalists or other writers that you find there are good examples of primary sources. Materials in newspapers also illustrate that sometimes the same document may be considered either a primary or a secondary source, depending on the use a historian makes of the source. For example, an April 8, 2003, article in the *New York Times* by Dexter Filkins reported a "Warm Welcome and Stubborn Resistance" as the U.S. First Marine Division completed its advance into Baghdad, Iraq.[6] This article might be a secondary source for an essay on the 2003 American offensive in Iraq, but it might as well be a primary source for an essay on the history of "embedded" journalists, participating in a U.S. Department of Defense experiment with wartime journalism. Understanding newspaper, and other, sources in this way will help you differentiate between secondary and primary sources for your topic.

Since good history essays should *always* refer to primary sources, you should be on the lookout for editions of the works by the various people who may enter your essay. Using materials written by those you write about gives your own work authority. When you use any edition of collected or selected works, check the dates of publication. Sometimes several different editions have been published of the same works. These editions may be of different sorts. The most valuable are editions of the complete works in which every surviving text is collected and indexed, sometimes with other materials from the time the person lived. These can be important to determine the different views of your subject either over time or when addressing different audiences.

Look for collections of speeches or sermons, published diaries, and editions of correspondence, all of which are also fairly common. Also read published (and, if they are available to you, unpublished) autobiographies, but

---

[6]Dexter Filkins, "Warm Welcome and Stubborn Resistance for Marines," *New York Times* April 8, 2003, p. A1.

be skeptical of them. Apply the same critical historical standards you would for any other source: Is the account *plausible, trustworthy, accurate*, and can it be *corroborated*? Remember, when anyone writes anything about themselves, they have a natural desire to shape their image for posterity. Autobiographies and memoirs almost always have a lot of fiction in them. Still, all of them contain some truth—although some are more truthful than others. The furor over James Frye's memoir, *A Million Little Pieces*, and his apparent invention of many details drew widespread attention to such problems not long ago. His defense, that the work contains "the emotional truth," was roundly criticized. Yet the problem is a real one, even for a historian writing a memoir, as historian Frank F. Mathias understood. Recounting his life as a young soldier during World War II in the South Pacific, Professor Mathias later admitted his *GI Jive: An Army Bandsman in World War II* was based upon "my memory, my letters, and some imagination to present a true picture."[7]

Perhaps this is why most historians enjoy reading such sources. Like photographs, they give us a sense of intimacy with bygone times and people we have not known and, like photographs, speeches, diaries, and letters, are frequently datable. You can quickly see that they belong to a certain time and place, and in the eternal flux of things, they seem to make time stand still for a moment. Sermons and speeches often give you a sense of the public image and message someone wanted to convey. Diaries and collections of letters, on the other hand, frequently reveal people in relatively unguarded prose, commenting on daily life without the caution that marks more public utterances. The private persona or personality of the diarist or letter writer may be different from the public image displayed in speeches or writing intended for a large audience. But take note: The historian—rather than the former soldier—Mathias also cautions that in a memoir, just as in photographs, sermons, diaries, speeches, and letters, "imagination must enhance truth."[8]

Often numerous sources relating to a general topic are collected and published in a form that may be readily available. One of the most monumental of these is *The War of the Rebellion: A Compilation of the Official Records of the Union and Confederate Armies*, published in seventy volumes a century ago and now available online at http://digital.library.cornell.

---

[7]Frank F. Mathias, "Writing a Memoir: The Involvement of Art with Craft," *The History Teacher* 19 (1986): 378.

[8]Mathias, 379.

edu/m/moawar/waro.html. The original volumes have an index; however, the search functions in the online edition are cumbersome to use. A newer CD-ROM version has better search options and contains additional related material. This vast resource almost seems to contain a transcription of nearly every scrap of paper exchanged within the armies on both sides in the Civil War, and there were many, indeed! The noise of battle during the Civil War was so tremendous that men under fire could not hear each other speak. Therefore written orders carried from place to place on the battle-field were much more common than in earlier wars, and thousands of these were collected by the editors.

We could list literally hundreds of additional examples of primary source collections that can help you in research, and many more of them are becoming available online or in other digital formats. Whatever your topic, check to see if you can locate a collection of documents related to your essay. When you search the library catalog, or use an Internet search engine, in addition to keywords for your topic, look for "sources" or "personal narratives" as an additional parameter; those are the principal terms used in Library of Congress subject headings to indicate primary source materials. Browse through the collections you find even if at first they don't seem related to your topic. You may be pleasantly surprised. But remember always to examine critically the primary sources that you do find.

Many museums, large and small, have collections of historic objects, which you might wish to use as sources for your essay as well. In the past few decades the number of such collections has grown tremendously. Many of them already have investigated these elements of material culture, which can help you in understanding how they relate to the topic of your essay. But like every source you might wish to use, you need to evaluate them carefully. As Professor Leora Auslander suggests in her article we mentioned in Chapter 1, you must consider not only "how people relate to objects," but also "the nature of the relation among words, images, and things...in particular historical contexts."[9] Rather than letting this dissuade you, consider it a challenge to expand your use of a wide variety of primary sources!

You may also find that your own college library has an archive or manuscript department with collections of unpublished letters, diaries, memos, and other materials. Look for them and see if there might

---

[9]Auslander, 1018.

be material related to your topic. Many libraries and archives now also include oral history collections, tapes, and records of people—both well known and obscure—discussing the past and their participation in past events. You can sometimes learn something by the tone of voice people use to describe past events, although other interviews may only be available in written transcripts. Or, for example, if you are writing about some aspect of combat in Korea, Vietnam, or perhaps even Iraq and Afghanistan, you may be able to find veterans willing to tell you of their experiences, giving you a firsthand view of history. The same is true of the civil rights movement in the United States, recent migrations within or from Europe, and many other events within memory of witnesses and participants still alive.

People who participated in great events or lived through particularly interesting times are often eager to talk about them. Don't be afraid to write or telephone people to ask for an interview, but by all means respect anyone who wants to remain silent if that is their wish. It is always best, however, to conduct interviews in person. Prepare for the interview by learning all you can about the person and by writing out questions beforehand. But don't be mechanically bound to your list after the interview begins. Explore each question thoroughly. Listen to your source and be prepared to ask for clarification of details. If possible, record your interview with your smartphone; if not, be sure to take extensive notes, clarifying and confirming any exact quotations you wish to record.

Many other primary sources for writing about history may also be found in abundance on the World Wide Web, some in less than obvious places. One historian recently confessed—if that is the correct word—to using the online auction site eBay as a location for research. Interested in popular expressions of northern sentiment during the Civil War, Jonathan White found several significant items for his research offered for sale by the "entrepreneurial junk collectors" among eBay dealers. White had not found these cards, covers, and broadsides through any database or Internet search, concluding that eBay offered "scholars a unique opportunity to consult or use items that they otherwise would never have discovered even after spending months searching through a multitude of library catalogs."[10] For some topics you might also find this to be true.

---

[10]Jonathan W. White, "An Unlikely Database: Using the Internet Creatively in Historical Research," *Perspectives: Newsmagazine of the American Historical Association* 44, no. 3 (March 2006): 53.

Although unorthodox, White's approach does offer a reminder that the World Wide Web can be a reservoir of potential sources of information. You may find some of these using the Internet search techniques we mentioned earlier in this chapter. As you will soon discover, many online sites offer primary source documents (sometimes along with secondary sources) for open public access, far too many to mention in this *Short Guide*. But if you want a place to begin a general exploration of some available materials, the many collections of the U.S. Library of Congress (http://loc.gov) offer a good place to start. You will find a great storehouse of source materials including manuscripts, print documents, photos, and also audio and video recordings. Although somewhat difficult to navigate, another starting point could be the Internet Archive of Texts and Documents. Through its original site, http://history.hanover.edu/texts.html, you will find a wide selection of documents in numerous categories as well as links to other excellent sites.

Both of these are stable sites, which you can depend on if you make citations to sources you find there. But we offer some words of caution. Web sites are changing all the time. Almost any excellent Web resource may disappear, either temporarily or for good. Even the valuable Internet archive kept by the Wayback Machine website (http://archive.org/web/web.php) remains amazingly incomplete. Of course everyone knows that books, too, are discarded, not least after extensive use. And archives may be destroyed in catastrophic events such as fire or through neglect. But somehow the transitory nature of the World Wide Web often looms larger in historians' minds. The Web is not yet a substitute for a good library. Do not let this concern lead you to avoid using it entirely. Use the Web cautiously. Take full advantage of the powers of available search engines to locate potential materials. Keep good records of what you find. And always go back to any site at least one additional time to be sure you have recorded the URL and other information correctly. Also learn to recognize that some problems in locating—and relocating—Web materials may be caused not at the source of the Web site but somewhere in the chain of transmission to the computer you are using.

As you look for primary sources, what you find online should be confirmation that such sources may also include a wide variety of materials including photographs, material objects, paintings, sculpture, and architecture. Liana Vardi's fine 1996 article, "Imagining the Harvest in Early Modern Europe," considers representations of peasants by artists for three centuries after 1500. She shows that the peasants—the farmers who worked the fields—gradually disappear from paintings of rural landscapes. By comparing paintings with poetry from the time, she argues that city dwellers and aristocrats became afraid of peasants, who frequently rebelled against the harsh conditions of their lives. Then, in the eighteenth century, peasants returned to the paintings, where they appear docile and obedient and happy.[11] The paintings, reproduced in black and white throughout the article, serve as essential primary sources for Professor Vardi's conclusions about popular attitudes centuries ago.

You, too, may find important visual sources for your own essays. Yet do not be lulled into thinking that all images, and especially photographs, can reproduce reality as you might imagine it. Alan Trachtenberg understood and explained this more than two decades ago in his article "Albums of War: On Reading Civil War Photographs." Many photographs of that war have shaped subsequent images of the conflict, but they are, Professor Trachtenberg wrote, "vulnerable to exactly the same obscurities of other forms of evidence. The simplest documentary questions of who did what, when, where, and why may be impossible to answer."[12] We could not agree more and, once again, encourage you to question *all* your sources, primary as well as secondary, and evaluate them carefully.

But at the same time, when considering primary sources for your essay, Professor Vardi's article should also remind you not to dismiss the possibilities of literature—poetry, short stories, and novels—which often capture the tenor and tone of the time in which they were written. While literary sources are sometimes difficult to interpret, particularly given the frequent metaphorical and occasionally personal expressions of the authors, in many cases the connections to a historical topic are clear enough. Consider, for example, this 1899 poem, "Take Up the White Man's Burden," by the well-known Anglo-Indian Rudyard Kipling, which he specifically headed "The United States and the Philippine Islands":

> Take up the White Man's burden—
>   Send forth the best ye breed—
> Go bind your sons to exile
>   To serve your captives' need;
> To wait in heavy harness
>   On fluttered folk and wild—
> Your new caught, sullen peoples,
>   Half devil and half child.
> . . . .

---

[11]Liana Vardi, "Imagining the Harvest in Early Modern Europe," *The American Historical Review* 101 (1996): 1357–1397.

[12]Alan Trachtenberg, "Albums of War: On Reading Civil War Photographs," *Representations* 9 (1985): 2–3.

> Take up the White Man's burden—
>   Ye dare not stoop to less—
> Nor call too loud on Freedom
>   To cloak your weariness;
> By all ye cry or whimper,
>   By all ye leave or do,
> The silent, sullen peoples
>   Shall weigh your Gods and you.[13]

Were you writing an essay on U.S. imperialism—or on imperialism and colonialism in general—the importance of this poem as a primary source should be clear. These brief verses capture some essential expressions of the colonial mentality of that era and, if nothing else, could lend an added dimension to your essay on the subject. Frequently you may come across literary works, perhaps some not so well known as Kipling's, which can serve to enliven what you write. You might need to do some additional reading to make certain your interpretation is not too far from the mark. Consider that effort, too, is a part of the evaluation process necessary before you use your sources for any history essay, and also as another example of the hard work that is required if you are to write well.

CONCLUDING YOUR RESEARCH

Even at this stage, you have not done all the preliminary work necessary to help in creating your essay. You may suppose that historians invariably follow these steps neatly one after the other. But remember our earlier advice! In practice things seldom run so smoothly. Historians may begin with one topic, discover another when they do research, and change their minds again when they start writing. As they write, they may redefine their topic, and as they redefine the topic they do more research. Writing down such thoughts often reveals gaps in your knowledge. So you go back to your research to fill in these gaps. And as you do research, you will find suggestions of other materials in what you read. As you gain more experience, you will find that writing is a process of leaping forward and leaping back, but above all involves some sort of writing as you begin research and continues until the essay is completed.

---

[13]Rudyard Kipling, "Take Up the White Man's Burden," in *A Choice of Kipling's Verse*, ed. T. S. Eliot (New York: Anchor Books, 1941), 143–144. There are many editions available.

You certainly will want to discover as many potential sources as possible, taking care to keep your *own* working bibliography from the start of your research, even when you are merely looking for potential sources. By starting early you will save yourself much grief. All too often students have come to us as they are completing the final version of a history essay asking for additional bibliographic information, including—on more than one occasion—the title of "that little green book" on their topic, or some other reference to a less than helpful description by which they have remembered a particular source. Your research bibliography should include complete information about the books, articles, Web sites, reference materials, and other sources you locate as well as to recommendations for further reading in the bibliographies appended to these sources. You may wish to jot the information down on your smartphone or similar device or even in a notebook kept for that purpose. Index cards, which we used when we began doing historical research, have been superseded by the note-taking capacity of computer programs and mobile applications such as *RefWorks, EndNote*, and *Noodle Tools*, which are primarily subscription services available in academic libraries, as well as more widely available options such as *Zotero* and *Mendeley* and the new mobile app, *Quick Cite*.

One advantage of some computer bibliography generation programs is that once you enter information for your references, the program will create the bibliography for you. This seems a wonderful convenience, but there is often a downside. Not all of the programs support the latest versions of the *Chicago Manual* and Turabian notes and bibliography citation formats common in historical writing. This can be especially important if you are using a wide variety of sources, including online materials. Given the power of word processing programs, though, if you become familiar with the basic information required in any citation—information about authorship, titles, locations, and dates—you can enter the details in a separate word processing file. Then you will have ready access to what you need for formatting your own bibliography—and notes!

But don't let the mechanics of your bibliographic efforts become a result in itself. To postpone writing until you have done all the possible research on the subject can be disastrous. Many historians have fallen before the demand they put on themselves to read one more book or article before they could start writing. That was the fate of Frederick Jackson Turner, who, after propounding his justly famous "frontier thesis" of American history, was expected to write many important books. He signed several contracts with publishers, happily accepting advances on expected royalties which he welcomed as a supplement to his modest faculty salary. Sadly, he produced only a single one of the expected books.

Despite managing to publish a few articles in academic journals, he finally confessed, "I hate to write," after numerous book deadlines had passed; "it is almost impossible for me to do so." Rather, he was caught up in research on numerous projects. He kept copious notes for many of them, while also collecting additional information about many other American history subjects he found interesting. "I have a lot of fun exploring, getting lost and getting back, and telling my companions about it," he admitted.[14] While delighting in informal conversations and academic debates, as well as extensive correspondence, concerning a wide array of topics, Turner seemed unable actually to complete the formal writing process for nearly all of his promised books.

Turner's difficulties in actually writing what was expected illustrates our fundamental belief about writing: At some point you simply have to settle down and do it! While basic curiosity might lead you to realize your research may never be fully completed, at some point you will need to conclude that aspect of the process. No matter how fascinating and satisfying your research, it takes a kind of courage that every historian must summon up if he or she is to complete the writing process. Use this checklist to help keep yourself on track as you search for information to help in writing your essay:

Writer's Checklist for Research

_____ ✔ Is my topic clearly focused?

_____ ✔ Have I looked widely for available reference materials related to the topic?

_____ ✔ Are the search terms I am using carefully chosen and refined?

_____ ✔ Am I using all the indexing tools available to me?

_____ ✔ Have I used the citations in my secondary sources to find other available materials?

_____ ✔ What primary sources related to the topic have I found?

_____ ✔ Does my working bibliography reflect all the available sources?

_____ ✔ Have I asked questions about and evaluated all my sources?

_____ ✔ Have I exercised sufficient discipline to write as my research is reasonably concluded

---

[14]Quoted in Richard Hofstadter, *The Progressive Historians* (New York: Knopf, 1968), 115–117; Hofstadter also provides a fuller account of Turner's difficulties in completing his writing projects.

NOTES AND DRAFTS

■ ■ ■

After studying this chapter, you should be able to
- Take useful notes for research and in class.
- Separate quotations and your own ideas in your notes.
- Organize your writing systematically.
- Use discipline in writing and revising drafts.
- Practice peer-editing of fellow students' writing.

Although every respectable historian knows the importance of gathering information before completing a historical essay, most also know how important it is to begin the writing process as early as possible. In reality, this is a form of practice. Pianists do finger exercises before they play. Baseball players take batting practice before a game. These activities help them limber up for the real thing. Similar exercises will help you prepare to write. Maintaining such a view of the writing process will also help you avoid falling victim to some common, and often recurring, myths about writing.

One such myth is that writers are inspired, that real writers turn out articles and books and reports with the greatest of ease. Another is that if you must write several drafts of anything, you are not a good writer. Still another is that if you labor to write what you want to say, you will not improve it much if you write a second or even a third draft. We can personally attest that none of these is really true in practice. While every writer has a different approach to the process, it is neither quick nor easy for any of them. All writing—if it is done well—is hard work.

For example, few writers manage to write without revising. The almost unanimous testimony of good writers in all disciplines is that writing is always difficult and that they must write several drafts to be satisfied with an essay or a book. "I write at least three drafts of everything," the celebrated American historian Richard Hofstadter confessed; "I have lots of second thoughts."[1] Indeed, the easier writing is to read, the harder it has been for the writer to produce it. Your final draft must express a clear understanding of your own thoughts. But the way to that understanding may lead through several drafts. The process of writing, taking notes, rereading, and revising clarifies your thoughts and strengthens your hold on your own ideas. Once you have gone through that process, you have an essay that cannot be blown away by the first person who comes along with a firm opinion.

Inexperienced writers often assume that an accomplished writer simply does all the research first and then writes. We may have unintentionally reinforced such a view by discussing research in some depth before turning to the writing, actually putting the words down. While that may be a useful structure for these ideas, we want to emphasize the ongoing close relationship between research and writing in reaching the finished product, your essay. Most experienced writers find that no matter how much they know about a subject at the start, the act of writing forces them to confront new problems and new questions, gives them new leads, sends them off in search of more information to pursue those new leads, and eventually takes them to conclusions different from those with which they began. For the experienced writer, the writing proceeds in a process of leaping forward and leaping back, but above all it involves some sort of writing very early and continuing until the essay is, in fact, completed.

RECORDING INFORMATION AND IDEAS

If you start writing early in the process, the great value of rewriting will be clearer to you. As you take notes during a lecture or discussion, listen carefully for important concepts, taking cues from repeated phrases, enumerated lists, and items presented in writing. Use quotation marks for key ideas stated briefly, but you should *not* try to take down every word. Instead always make an effort to focus on what is most important. After class, try to summarize what you heard and consolidate your understanding of the most important concepts. Write down any questions you have

---

[1]Quoted in David S. Brown, *Richard Hofstadter: An Intellectual Biography* (Chicago: University of Chicago Press, 2007), 120.

about the information; many instructors will entertain your questions—in later classes or during individual consultations—and attempt to help you understand more clearly what they want you to know. Write down those answers as well! Also try writing a brief summary of the important points made; that process alone may lead you back to update certain sections of your notes. It will likely lead you as well to formulate further ideas about what you have just heard. This active note-taking process will be a great help as you study for tests, especially when you begin preparation for essay examinations. And such a writing habit may also produce a personal treasure trove of topics for future history essays.

Note-taking from your reading and research, however, will be even easier. As you are reading, you can go back and reread, concentrating on what was not clear to you at first. Always work on identifying the major points, separating them from supporting arguments and subsidiary evidence. Take extra care to use quotation marks for any direct statements you want to remember, but keep even those to a minimum. Always try to summarize in your own words. As an example, consider this brief passage from the well-regarded book *Sweetness and Power: The Place of Sugar in Modern History*, by Sidney Mintz:

> When it was first introduced into Europe around 1100 a.d., sugar was grouped with spices—pepper, nutmeg, mace, ginger, cardamom, coriander, galingale (related to ginger), saffron, and the like. Most of these were rare and expensive tropical (and exotic) imports, used sparingly by those who could afford them at all. In the modern world, sweetness is not a "spice taste," but is counterposed to other tastes of all kinds (bitter as in "bittersweet," sour as in "sweet and sour," piquant as in "hot sausage" and "sweet sausage"), so that today it is difficult to view sugar as a condiment or spice. But long before most north Europeans came to know of it, sugar was consumed in large quantities as a medicine and spice in the eastern Mediterranean, in Egypt, and across North Africa. Its medical utility had already been firmly established by physicians of the time—including Islamized Jews, Persians, and Nestorian Christians, working across the Islamic world from India to Spain—and it entered slowly into European medical practice via Arab pharmacology.
>
> As a spice sugar was prized among the wealthy and powerful of western Europe, at least from the Crusades onward. By "spice" is meant here that class of "aromatic vegetable productions," to quote Webster's definition, "used in cooking to season food and flavor sauces, pickles, etc." We are accustomed not to thinking of sugar as spice, but, rather, to thinking of "sugar *and* spice." This habit of mind attests to the significant changes in the use and meanings of sugar, in the relationship between

sugar and spices, and in the place of sweetness in western food systems that have occurred since 1100.[2]

Here are some notes taken by one student after reading this passage:

—sugar introduced to Europe ca. 1100 ad, grouped with spices—rare & expensive tropical imports, used sparingly by those who could afford them

—now sweetness not a "spice taste," but compared to other tastes—"bittersweet," "sweet and sour," or "hot sausage" & "sweet sausage"

—before Europeans knew of sugar consumed as medicine and spice in eastern Mediterranean, Egypt, & North Africa

—physicians—Islamized Jews, Persians, and Nestorian Christians in Islamic world from India to Spain—used sugar as medicine, slowly came to European medical practice via Arab pharmacology

—as spice, sugar prized by wealthy and powerful of western Europe since Crusades

—Webster's dictionary: "spice" "aromatic vegetable productions used in cooking to season food and flavor sauces, pickles, etc."

—we think of sugar not as spice, but of "sugar *and* spice"

—shows significant changes in use and meaning of sugar, in relationship between sugar and spices, and in place of sweetness in western food systems since 1100

These notes, however, would be of limited value. They are nearly 60 percent as long as the original excerpt and little more than a sequential listing of what appeared there; the note-taker does not appear to have thought carefully about the reading. Moreover, these notes often repeat words and phrases, sometimes pieced together in the same or a similar order, directly from the original, but without the benefit of quotation marks. Using these notes in the preparation of an essay could easily lead

---

[2]Sidney W. Mintz, *Sweetness and Power: The Place of Sugar in World History* (New York: Viking, 1985), 79–80.

to your being accused of plagiarism, an unpardonable sin for any writer. Much better if you tried to read the original passage, summarize its main points and, at the same time, indicate in your notes—by using quotation marks—any key quotations you might later use in an essay. Now consider this example of notes made after reading, and then rereading, the same passage from Professor Mintz's book:

```
Mintz, Sweetness, pp. 79-80

    Sugar long seen as medicine by Muslim, Jew-
ish, and Nestorian physicians in Islamic lands;
became known in Europe after Crusades (ca. 1100)
as a spice and was regarded just as valuable. Hard
for moderns to see it that way: "We are accustomed
not to thinking of sugar as spice, but, rather,
to thinking of 'sugar and spice.'" (80) Changing
perceptions of sweetness also seen in contrast to
other tastes: "bittersweet" and "sweet and sour"
```

Notice how this second set of notes attempts to capture both the historical sequence of events *and* the main idea of the original passage. They also indicate clearly, in an abbreviated reference, the source of all the information and, more specifically, the exact reference for the quotation. Taking notes such as these from the very beginning will serve as an early start for any writing process. And you may well benefit from taking notes such as these as you read required texts in your history classes as well, not just for essay examinations, but also in being better prepared for lectures and class discussions.

As you read background information, and later specific sources, regarding your essay topic, you should certainly keep notes with location information, including URLs for Web sources and page numbers for books and articles. The location details will help you find the information again should you need it. Make note of questions about what you read, much as you would when you take notes during your classes. (We often scribble notes and questions in the margins of our own books. But never, NEVER write in a library book, or any book you have borrowed!) There are now many ways to keep such notes. For years students and scholars used notecards or notebooks, organized separately for each project; one of us still has nearly ten boxes of notecards used in writing his doctoral dissertation! In recent years, however, we have come to rely more and more on our computers for note-taking as well as writing. We encourage you to do so as well, or even to take advantage of applications for keeping up with your research on your portable digital devices.

While you may use almost any word processing program to accomplish such tasks, there are a number of specific note-taking programs available that you may wish to consider instead. Some, such as *RefWorks* or *EndNote* available in some libraries, are primarily intended for collecting bibliographic information. The similar *NoodleTools* suggests it can also accommodate notes, but clearly bibliographic information dominates its instructional messages. A new mobile application *Quick Cite* (not to be confused with an operation of the same name within *Noodle Tools*) also allows you to scan barcodes from books and have full citations delivered to your e-mail. Perhaps the best and most widely available research data programs are the free, open source *Zotero* (at http://www.zotero.org) or the commercial program *Mendeley* (at http://www.mendeley.com). You can find a helpful video comparing the two, as well as some user instruction files, on the Portland State University library website (at http://guides.library.pdx.edu/managecitations). There are new, inexpensive apps available for scanning book barcodes into *Zotero* (*BibUp* [at http://elearning.unifr.ch/bibup/tuto/] for iPhone or *Scanner for Zotero* [at https://play.google.com/store/apps/details?id=org.ale.scanner.zotero] for Android phones), and no doubt other apps for both programs will soon become available. Some other note-taking programs that prominently feature collaboration functions, such as those in *Debrief* and *OneNote*, are better suited to business applications or at least for multi-author projects.

Whether you use a specialized note-taking or database program or merely take notes with your usual word processing program, be sure to save your notes as you work and especially as you finish each research or writing session, no matter how short. Some programs automatically create backup files, but we encourage you to make others. Take advantage of the easy means electronic media provide to save your work. Keep several copies using your computer or mobile device as well as additional copies in other formats. For as long as we've been writing and teaching, we've heard disheartening experiences almost every year of tribulations students and colleagues have undergone because they have lost all their research due to one sort of disaster or another. We have not wanted to join them! In preparing each edition of this book, for example, we've kept copies of every chapter in separate files and have four or more copies of each—on our computer hard drives, CD-ROMs created with our computers, USB (or flash) drives, "cloud" storage sites, as well as printed paper versions. You should do so, too, even with the notes from your first inquiries into potential topics, and continue as you proceed with more intensive research.

Whatever format you select, the main point is to take notes even as you begin your investigations. Ask yourself questions. And while they are still fresh in your mind, jot down a few possible—yet plausible—answers. Put down significant phrases. Note places where your sources disagree. Pay attention to what one historian notices and another ignores. Make notes of your own opinions about both the historians and the material. Even in the early stages of your research, important ideas may pop into your head. Record them on your mobile device or with a computer, and then test them with further study. Your subsequent research may confirm that some of your first impressions are gems!

Whether you write notes by hand, type on your computer with a word processor or another note-taking program, or enter them into your smart phone or tablet, you would do well to keep five key principles for note-taking in mind. Doing so will save you time in the long run and save you from making any number of writing errors. Here is a review of those principles with examples from the notes Penny Sonnenburg made as she wrote her essay on manifest destiny:

1. Keep an Ongoing Bibliography

As we suggested in the last chapter, you should keep a working bibliography in your notes from the beginning and throughout your research. Take special care to include the essential elements of information for each reference you consult, recorded in a separate entry. Each should include all of the following: *authorship* (and also the names of editors and/or translators); the *title* (or titles, in the case of an article in a book or journal); the *location* where you found the information (including the publisher and the place of publication of books or, in the case of Internet information, the URL, and—when appropriate—volume and page numbers); and the *date(s)* of publication and/or access. As you begin, it is not necessary to follow the conventions or precise patterns from *The Chicago Manual*, or Turabian's short guide, for note or bibliographic formats. But it is very important to be sure you include all the essential details. For example, you might consult:

```
Adams, Ephraim Douglass. The Power of Ideals in
American History. AMS Press, New York, 1969.
```

This information will need to be reorganized when you write in a conventional bibliographic or other reference format, but the first principle for any note-taking effort is clear: *Be sure you record where you got your information.*

If you make sure to record all the bibliographic details as you start with any source, later on you can refer in your notes simply to the author and a shortened title plus page (and volume) numbers. Were you using Adams's *The Power of Ideals in American History* as a source in research about the origins of manifest destiny, as did Penny Sonnenburg for her essay presented in Appendix A, you might also write (as she did) "Adams, *Ideals*, 67" (to indicate *Ideals* as the essence of the source title and 67 as the page number). Since you must be able to refer accurately to your sources when you write, you must also do so when you take notes. You will save yourself much grief if you keep track of your sources carefully while you do your research!

2. Carefully Select Keywords

An important second principle for note-taking involves selecting appropriate keywords and using them in your note files. After reading Frederick Merk's *Manifest Destiny and Mission in American History*, you would want to take specific note of the author's overall thesis, as did Ms. Sonnenburg:

```
Merk, Manifest Destiny, [thesis]        nationalism,
                                        expansion


making worldwide comparisons, the author
establishes that territorial expansion, known in
the US as "manifest destiny," was an important part
of American nationalism
```

You can later locate all the references you have found on a particular subject with the search or FIND function on your word processing or note-taking program to locate those key words even in a large file with many notes for your essay. Many such programs will also allow you to shift your notes to the electronic file in which you are writing your essay; simply block and copy text from your note files, then open your essay file, and paste the information there. Be sure to indicate clearly [perhaps in square brackets] location information, particularly Web links or page numbers, as you write your notes into a computer file. For some Web sites, you must indicate clearly the precise and complete URL for the particular source you have found, as well as any search terms you have used to locate specific information.

3. Avoid Copying Quotations

A third key principle for good note-taking is to avoid copying direct quotations in your notes. Writing down or even copying the quotation takes time, and you can easily make errors in transcribing it. You save time—and sometimes create your own best writing—if you exercise your mind by summarizing or paraphrasing rather than merely copying a direct quotation. You may wish to photocopy or make digital scans of some pages relevant to your work, especially if you must return the book before writing the paper. But heed this warning: Do not simply stash all the copies in a folder or file with all your other research! Instead, persevere and make notes while the purpose of the source is still fresh in your mind. Writing down ideas in your own words from the beginning is especially valuable. It opens your mind to the possibilities of how you might present the information when you begin to write your essay. And be especially careful in attempting to paraphrase: Do not slip in copying the original with only minor changes involving just a couple of words or using the same structure of presenting ideas.

As you read Adams's *The Power of Ideals in American History,* you might make a note such as this, which Ms. Sonnenburg created, summarizing some of his views, as follows:

```
Adams, Ideals, [67]                              origins

provides background knowledge to understand the
true beginnings of manifest destiny, not just in
American history.
```

Notice the inclusion of a separate topic heading, "origins"; this is especially helpful if you are using note cards or writing notes in the margins of a separate notebook. You can also use such headings as key words in computerized notes to find materials on particular aspects of your subject within a saved file. When you begin writing your complete essay, you can return to the original source (or your photocopies) for additional details and quote exactly if that then seems necessary.

4. Keep Any Quotations Separate

If you do find a few essential direct quotations that are especially significant to your research, keep in mind the fourth principle for note-taking: Always take special care in making copies of direct quotations. You will avoid additional effort later by *always* placing direct quotations within quotation marks in your notes. Also review the quotation for accuracy once you've first written it down. The eye and the hand can slip while you are looking first at your source and then at your paper, computer, or portable digital device. It may help to put a check or asterisk (*) by the quotation to tell yourself that you have reviewed it for accuracy once you have put it down.

Here is another note, including a direct quotation, from those made by Ms. Sonnenburg for her essay concerning manifest destiny; this is from another source discussing some of the historical origins of the idea:

```
Barker, Traditions, [312]          natural law/destiny

* The large and somewhat general expression "became
a tradition of human civility which runs continu-
ously from the Stoic teachers of the Porch to the
American Revolution of 1776 and the French Revolu-
tion of 1789."
```

Notice how she has used the * symbol to identify a quotation in this note. This particular quotation may seem a particularly apt explanation of natural law—although the words themselves may reflect historical writing of more than a half-century ago—than it is to a direct quote addressing manifest destiny itself. Try to take such matters into consideration and use direct quotations only sparingly in your notes as well as your essays.

5. Record Your Own Ideas

Get in a regular habit of including your own comments and ideas as you read and make notes; that's an important final principle for note-taking. Commenting requires you to reflect on what you read, making you an active rather than a passive reader. *But be sure to distinguish between the notes that are your own thoughts and notes that are direct quotations or summaries of your sources.* We often put an arrow, like this ➡, before our own thoughts whether we are using cards, a notebook, or our computers. The arrow lets us know that these thoughts are ours. If you do not take care in distinguishing your thoughts from the thoughts of your source, you may be accused of plagiarism, a very serious matter and one from which few authors can easily recover.

Here is an example of how Ms. Sonnenburg made a note about her own thoughts on the origins of manifest destiny, clearly marking it as her own idea, as we suggested:

chosen people

➡ the belief in manifest destiny has mostly appeared to be a uniquely American characteristic, but further research on other countries and their "chosen people" concepts leads to belief that the concept of manifest destiny predated not only United States history, but in some cases even also predated United States existence as a country

The purpose of such a note is to keep your mind active as you read. Again, notice the inclusion of a topic heading, which will lead you back to your own ideas as well as other information in your notes on the same topic. This practice will also help you shape ideas for the essay that you are writing. And as you begin research, and several times during the process, you may wish to review this checklist as a reminder:

Writer's Checklist for Taking Notes

_____ ✔ Do I practice note-taking when in class and reading assigned texts?

_____ ✔ Have I recorded full bibliographic information for each source?

_____ ✔ Am I careful to record all appropriate keywords in my notes?

_____ ✔ Do I limit the number of direct quotations in my notes?

_____ ✔ Have I used my own words to summarize or paraphrase information I find?

_____ ✔ Have I taken special care in recording any direct quotations?

_____ ✔ Have I looked for patterns, even unexpected, in the evidence?

_____ ✔ Are my own ideas a part of my notes on the subject?

ORGANIZING YOUR ESSAY

Taking notes that focus on both information and ideas—including your *own* ideas—will help you begin putting your mind to work organizing your essay. Having spent some time refining your subject, gathering a bibliography, doing preliminary reading, and taking notes, you should feel more confident about your knowledge. You will have moved beyond the somewhat flat and limited accounts of the encyclopedias and other reference books, and you will have started looking at specialized books and articles as well as primary sources related to your topic. You will have been asking questions along the way, writing them down in your notes. You will have noticed patterns or repeated ideas in your research, and you should have jotted down some of your own ideas as well. In these ways, your note-taking process should have helped you find interesting approaches to your topic.

Sometimes a pattern occurs in a consistent response to certain subjects. For example, the notion of manifest destiny was prevalent and commonly used outside the United States. Which nations also employed and extensively used this notion? How far back can one logically trace the idea of manifest destiny? As did Ms. Sonnenburg, you may have started with the resolve to write an essay about manifest destiny. If you were lucky, you thought of a limited topic right away, one you might do in ten or fifteen pages. Perhaps, however, you were not able to limit your topic enough. Try making a list of interesting topics or problems relating to manifest destiny. Keep working at it until you arrive at something manageable. The following notes she used illustrate this attempt to produce both something interesting and something you can do in the time and space available.

> "Manifest Destiny and its importance in world history."
>
> —Too vague. Not focused enough with too many subtopics.
>
> "Manifest Destiny and its influence in European history."
>
> —A narrower focus, yet still encompasses much.
> —European history covers too large a span to incorporate into a paper of this size.

```
"Manifest Destiny: The American Dream of
Expansionism"

—too narrow does not recognize motivation for
 the topic, ignores the true question of its
 origins.
```

For this last topic the temptation might be to go from manifest destiny to the American ideology of expansionism. Then you need to ask questions such as those Ms. Sonnenburg considered: Do I want this paper to be about the various stages of American expansion? Does this topic completely overlook the world influence of manifest destiny? Has my initial research been directed more at a global overview? In essence, What do I want to prove by writing this essay? What are other historical explanations of manifest destiny? As you ask questions like these, look back over your research notes and see if you can detect a pattern. Slowly an idea emerges and you add it to the list of potential topics.

```
"Manifest Destiny: A Requirement for All
Nations."

—widespread evidence of this, but still a narrow
 focus.
—considerable primary source information in newspa-
 per articles, plus Internet sources provide trans-
 lated material.
```

Now you have a starting point, a provisional title. Remember, though, you can change anything at this stage, and your changes may be sweeping. While you use it, the provisional title will give direction to your work. That sense of direction will help you work faster and more efficiently because it helps organize your thoughts, making you evaluate information you have collected so you can make proper use of it. If you have done your research well, you cannot use all the information you have collected in your notes. Good writing is done out of an abundance of knowledge. The provisional title will act as a filter for your mind. It will help you organize things you should keep for your essay and let information go that will not contribute to your argument.

Once you arrive at a provisional title, refocus your reading. If you plan to write about the origins of manifest destiny, limit yourself to reading historians' explanations of the concept and philosophical works that underlay the concept. You may be so interested in manifest destiny that you decide to continue to seek more information about the use of the idea in American history to justify taking Mexican land with an eye even farther south. Good! But while you are working on this essay, limit your reading to information that helps you to your goal. Maintaining that discipline will help you avoid the problems (mentioned in the last chapter) which plagued the famous historian Frederick Jackson Turner! We would also encourage you to write at least a brief outline to help organize your ideas and your evidence.

Some writers sit down and start hammering on the keyboard without any clear idea of the steps they will take in developing their argument. Others worry about the details of formal outlining—Roman numerals, large and small, and the placement of each point or subpoint within the outline—just as they might have been taught early in school. But either approach may distract you from the essential task. Then your effort to frame an outline would become just another insurmountable obstacle that keeps you from writing.

Instead, focus on organizing your thoughts. Most people find it more efficient to shape their ideas in some way before they begin to write a draft, and we have found that to be true in our writing. We encourage you to do the same, even for short essays and before you start writing your answers for an essay examination. You can at least jot down a list of points you want to cover—a list that can be much more flexible than a detailed outline.

This need for structure has long been recognized as a cornerstone for historical prose. More than a half-century ago, the American cultural historian Dixon Wecter extolled the virtues of careful organization, observing that the historian's "structural gift—not merely the lumping together of details to be hurled at the reader like a soggy snowball—yields writing that can be read with pleasure." But his praise for the well-organized essay came with a caution, that "the structure ought to be clean and firm, yet not obtruding the bones of its skeleton."[3] You owe it to your readers to shape your essay with such a goal in mind. Organize the key ideas for your essay so that their connections are readily apparent yet presented as something more than a sequential list of topics.

As you work on enumerating your key points, let your intuition suggest other, perhaps better, forms of organization. Never be afraid to change an outline once you have begun. But no matter how clearly you think you see your project in outline before you, write a full draft! Writing

---

[3]Dixon Wecter, "How to Write History," in *A Sense of History: The Best Writing from the Pages of "American Heritage"* (New York: ibooks, 2003), 43; Wecter's essay, originally titled "History and How to Write It," appeared in the August 1957 issue of *American Heritage* magazine.

may change your ideas. Be ready to follow your mind in its adventures with the evidence. Remember that you are taking your readers on a journey, not a laborious recitation of loosely related facts and information somehow coalesced to read like an essay. You might create a rough outline something like the one Ms. Sonnenburg constructed for her essay on the origins of manifest destiny:

> Argument: John O'Sullivan's editorial about manifest destiny leads one to believe that it was an American concept to rationalize the expansionist movement that was sweeping the United States during the hotly debated annexation of Texas. But other nations before the United States embraced the notion in their own expansionist movements.
>
> 1. John O'Sullivan's editorial itself supports the idea of the citizens of the United States being a selected people
> 2. Perspectives and explanations of natural law/ right and how it can be related to manifest destiny
> 3. Early historians' viewpoints on the importance of using similar ideas in solidifying nationalism
> 4. Anglo-Saxon ideas of manifest destiny as essential for national survival
> 5. Global analogies
> 6. Early national precedents in the United States (up to 1840)
> 7. "Manifest Destiny" term popularized, 1840s
> 8. Extension to sea power and the Pacific Basin

A simple outline such as hers avoids a proliferation of unnecessary numbers and letters for headings and subheadings. You may add subheadings if you want, but you may not need them. Determining the sequence of your thoughts is most important and likely sufficient. Having made an outline such as this, you can more confidently write a first draft. In this case you would have decided to shape an analytical essay looking at manifest destiny from a more global perspective. You will explain the origins of the concept, shape a narrative of its articulation and use, introduce explanations of other concepts relating to it, and explain why it is important to attempt to overlook limitations on the subject. Along the way you will explain who wrote about these concepts. And you can then actually begin writing a draft of your full essay.

Penny Sonnenburg used just such a process in creating her essay, taking notes and organizing ideas before actually writing a draft. Read her final essay in Appendix A; try to see how she proceeded in her work as we have described. Of course, her first efforts at writing this history essay may not have proceeded as carefully and systematically as we have suggested. It is likely yours will not either. But working from notes, to a sketch map or even a "storyboard" of your essay, will help you improve the final result. And we cannot emphasize enough that working this way takes practice. You will benefit from trying it more than once!

Writing and Revising Drafts

Every time you do so, you will still need to leave yourself enough time to work on several drafts of your paper. If you start writing an essay the day before it is due, stay up all night to finish that first draft, and hand it in without having time to revise it, you do an injustice to yourself and your instructor. You may get by, but you may not be proud of your work, and the instructor will probably be bored with it. A hard-pressed instructor, sitting up for hours and hours reading and marking papers from everyone in the class (and yes, we have actually done this!), deserves your best effort.

We are not saying you should avoid staying up all night long working on your paper before you hand it in. Many writers discover that they get an adrenaline flow from working steadily at a final draft for hours and hours before they give it up, and they may stay up nearly all night because they are excited about their work and cannot leave it. We understand that feeling from our own writing adventures. Hearing the birds begin to sing outside at first light before dawn after working at our yellow pads or keyboard all night long is an experience we have both shared, and we have liked it. That kind of night comes when we have worked hard for a long time, perhaps for years, and feel in command of what we are doing and want to drive on to the end.

But no writer can produce consistently good work by waiting until the last minute to begin. Discipline yourself. If you have difficulty starting to write, make a concerted effort to actually write for some short period of time, even ten or fifteen minutes. Then stop, consult your notes, and take a break. Come back as soon as you can; reread what you have written. Often reading over your work will stimulate further thought—and writing! Although you may not go very fast at first, try not to become discouraged. After a night's sleep, begin again. The most important task in writing your first draft is actually to write it! Get a beginning, a middle, and an end down on paper or on your computer. Write more than you need to write at first. If your assignment is to write fifteen pages, make your first draft twenty pages. Pack in information. Perhaps use a very few select quotations. Ruminate about what you are describing. Ask yourself the familiar questions about your paper—*Who? What? When? Where? Why?* and also *How?*—and try to answer them.

As you go from your notes and outline to writing a draft of your essay, take special care when using your word processing program. In particular, the ease of block and click operations for capturing and moving electronic text from one file (or even a Web page) to another can be a temptation for including large segments of a source in your notes—and then into your essay. Hence our suggestions that you take special care if you do include quotations in your notes! Failing to do so could lead to careless insertion of some material you have copied directly into your essay. And if you are careless, you will be guilty of plagiarism. Remember: It is *your* responsibility to avoid such errors.

When you get your first draft finished, you'll feel an immense relief; an unwritten assignment is more formidable than one you have written—even in a rough draft. You now have some idea what you can say in the space you have available. You have some idea of the major questions you want to address. You know some areas of weakness where you have to do further research. You can see which of your conclusions seem fairly certain and which seem shaky. You have an idea of your overall thesis, a controlling argument that resolves or defines some puzzle that you find in your sources. And you can now revise and in the process eliminate the extra words and sentences you packed into your first draft.

Writers have long made revisions, even marking on their first drafts. Manuscripts of many well-known nineteenth- and twentieth-century authors reveal such tinkering with their work, crossing out passages, adding others, writing new text in the margins, until the manuscripts are nearly impossible to read. Then they had to start again on a fresh piece of paper! But no matter how messy, they saved the originals (as their archived papers attest) so they might go back and look again at their initial writing efforts.[4]

Computer word processing programs, of course, have made that process easier. But often the original inspirations are gone, erased from the screen and replaced by a new version. We've found this to be a particular problem in our writing and have taken to saving several versions of electronic drafts. Sometimes we open a new window on our computers and work separately on what seems to be a troublesome passage. Then we save that as a separate file so we can go back and look at it again. With the vast digital storage capacity of modern electronic devices, we can save many of these, but we are careful to give each a distinct file name. And we are grateful that our computers date and time each saved file so we are able, if necessary, to reconstruct the sequence of our thoughts. We believe the potential of our electronic writing tools—even more than the quick availability of information on the Internet—marks perhaps the greatest contributions of our electronic age to the writing of historians.

Some writers prefer to print out a draft and go over it with a pen or pencil, making changes that they then type into the draft on the computer. Others are more comfortable revising directly on their computer screens. You should use the method, or combination of methods, that suits you best. Keep in mind, though, that the most important part of the task is to read your work with a self-critical eye. You can cultivate a good sense of revision by reading your own work again and again. Be sure you consider, or reconsider, some of the steps you have already used in the process. As you read, ask yourself questions related to the five basic principles for writing a good history essay (which we discussed in Chapter 1):

1. Is my essay sharply focused on a limited topic?
2. Does it have a clearly stated argument?
3. Is it built, step by step, on carefully acknowledged evidence?
4. Does it reflect my own dispassionate thoughts?
5. Is it clearly written with an intended audience in mind?

---

[4]There are several examples featured in a recent *Psychology Today* blog post; Jonathan Gottschall, "Crappy First Drafts of Great Books," 27 March 2012, http://www.psychologytoday.com/blog/the-storytelling-animal/201203/crappy-first-drafts-great-books, accessed 11 July 2013.

And, of course, ask yourself once again, Does the essay represent my own original work?

Consider all these questions carefully as you read your draft. Reading aloud helps. You can sometimes pick out rough places in your prose because they make you stumble in reading them. Reading aloud with inflection and expression will help you catch places where you may be misleading or confusing. You probably want to take full advantage of the many features of an electronic writing program to revise and improve what you have written. Yet no such program, no matter how advanced or up-to-date, will be helpful until you learn how to use it effectively! Many colleges and universities have adopted particular word processing programs as a standard for their campuses and frequently provide technical assistance in using them. Take advantage of such help. Rather than an indication of your ignorance, doing so is a signal of your intent to improve your writing. Recent editions of word processing programs often have very useful help menus or utilities included. Take full advantage of them, as well, both to learn how the program works and to refresh your memory about features you infrequently use.

But it isn't necessary to master all the features before you begin to write. At a minimum, though, you will want to know how to use **bold** or *italic* text, set margins, change fonts, insert special characters (such as the currency symbols £, ¥, and €), add page numbers, and, of course, insert footnotes (and endnotes). We are grateful that our word processors allow us to change our citations from footnotes to endnotes and back again. You will be, too, if you first used one format and then discover your instructor would prefer another. We have found, however, that occasionally the automatic formatting of footnotes (much more so than endnotes) may result in awkward placement of references. You may need to manually alter the number of lines of text on a page to adjust the placement of the notes. If you do not have someone who can assist you in mastering these functions, try the program's help features, an online instruction site, or your campus computer help service. The time you spend will be well rewarded with an essay that looks and reads as you really want it to.

We have appreciated the great advantage our computers and word processing programs have been in allowing us to revise our essays; not only moving text, but also correcting errors, is far easier than we recall from an era of typewriters, paper, erasers, and correction fluid. Frequently the newer programs will do some of this automatically, or almost automatically, for you. But we caution you to take care in using such features. Often the programs are designed to make such changes with minimal, if any, input from the writer. Likewise some programs or apps automatically create bibliographic entries. But these, too, require your careful scrutiny before you use them. Remember: *You* are responsible for what appears in the final version of your essay. So be certain that any such changes reflect what *you* want to say. If you can set which items may be autocorrected, do so. If you cannot, you may wish to turn off any autocorrect functions. In any case, always read over the final text of your essay and edit it yet again yourself before you submit it to your instructor.

The word processing programs we use—and likely yours as well—are also invaluable for checking our spelling, but only against the words stored in their memories. If you can add words to the spell checker, by all means do so; that way special terms associated with your topic will not be marked as misspelled. But be careful when you enter those words. Make sure the spelling you wish to use is the one you actually save. We always read what we have written on the screen and study each of the errors identified by the program. We urge you to do the same. Most often we correct those the computer has spotted. But we also know that in the binary logic of the computer, some mistakes are not readily identified. For example, if you refer to a particular *sight* where you have found valuable sources for your essay, that will not be marked as misspelled, even though your instructor may wonder why you were searching for something you could see out your window rather than on a Web *site*. There are many other examples.

Other word processing innovations may not be as useful to you in the writing process. Among these, grammar-checking functions are one of those that can be both helpful and also mystifying. When we've changed a word from singular to plural and forgotten to change the corresponding verb, the program usually marks the error, and we appreciate that. But sometimes whole phrases are noted as problematic, which, on close examination, seem to be exactly as we intended and easily read. Also the thesaurus on our word processors frequently offers only limited options for potential synonyms, so we would suggest that you turn instead to an online version of the venerable *Roget's Thesaurus*, first published in 1852, available at http://education.yahoo.com/reference/thesaurus. By far, our least favorite word processing innovation is the auto-summarizing option, which seldom achieves anything like the "executive summary" it promises. We never use this option, preferring to make our own summaries of what we have written if they are needed, and we urge you to do the same.

After rereading our essays and making revisions on our computer screens, we have come back to the practice of also printing out a manuscript, going over it carefully with pen or pencil, and only then inserting final corrections and revisions in the computer. You may wish to consider this approach as well. But above all, you must take special care to read your work over multiple times. Professional writers often have others read their work and make suggestions as well. Get help from friends—as we have for every edition of this book. Do not ask them, "What do you think of my essay?" They will tell you it is good. Ask them instead, "What do you think I am saying in this paper?" You will sometimes be surprised by what comes out—and you will get some ideas for revision. Also ask them what you might do to improve your writing so that the essential points you want to make would be clear to them.

Some of you may also be involved in a peer editing process in which students comment on drafts of one anothers' essays. Your college or university may foster such collaborations, or your instructor may encourage—or even require—you to do so. If not, you may wish to form your own group— a kind of writing club—in which you will all help one another in revising your essays. Recent additions to word processing programs may also facilitate revisions through peer editing and similar processes. Sometimes called "track changes," these features permit several people to read each document file and make suggested deletions, insertions, and comments—each using distinctive colors for their recommendations.

As the author, you may want to ask several friends to read a computer file with your essay and make electronic editorial suggestions. If they do so sequentially, each adding new advice, you can come back to your essay in a single file with a variety of comments and ideas for improving what you have written. Most such programs then allow you to accept or reject each of those changes and incorporate decisions about them into your final document. This sort of collaborative writing and revision process does take some getting used to, but it has the advantage of easily consolidating comments and making it relatively easy to incorporate them into your final draft. We encourage you to explore this word processing innovation as a means of making easier the peer editing process we also strongly recommend.

There are a number of explanations and guides to the process of peer editing, many available online. One that our students have found helpful is in the "Guilford Writing Manual," prepared a number of years ago for students at Guilford College by Professor Jeff Jeske and revised in recent years. It can be found at http://library.guilford.edu/peer-editing. In addition, the ten questions in the "Writer's Checklist for Peer Editing" at the end of this chapter offer an effective approach you can use in the process.

If you do take advantage of this frequently useful approach in your revision process, keep in mind that the purpose is to help one another, not

to demonstrate how much more you may think you know about writing—
or the topic of the essay—than the author. A critical eye in the revision
process is not just about making criticisms! As Professor Jeske cautions:

> It is worth remembering that a major goal of peer editing is to enable
> writers to make effective revising decisions. Praise alone will not help;
> when it appears unalloyed, it suggests that the editor has not invested
> the necessary effort, not thought deeply about the paper's effects and
> the way the prose could be improved.
>
> Nevertheless, the tone of the editorial response should be
> positive. Don't merely point out what's wrong. Identify the things
> that the author has done well: this way the author will know what to
> continue....
>
> The collective goal is that we all improve—and ... that we develop
> a positive attitude toward the activity in which we are engaged.[5]

You will likely find that helping others with their writing will also sharpen
your ability to improve your own drafts as you reread and revise them.

For most writers, the process of improving drafts goes on until the
last minute. Writing and revising drafts will help you focus on all parts of
your work more clearly. It will help you see your thinking, your research,
your factual knowledge, your expression, and the shape of your ideas. Very
often as you write and rewrite drafts of your essay, you will realize that your
thought is flabby or you may suddenly think of contrary arguments you
have not thought of before. You can then revise to take these contrary arguments into account. Reading your work over and over again, and taking
advantage of comments from others, will help you track your own ideas so
that they might flow from one to another without leaving gaps that might
hinder readers from making the connections you want them to make.

Finally, we again want to encourage you at each stage in your writing
process—from initial inquiries, through your research on a particular topic,
as you prepare drafts of your essay, and in revising as you complete the
final version of your essay—to make backup copies of your work. Too often
students have come to us ashen-faced, reporting they have lost, erased, or
destroyed the only disk on which they saved their essay. While we can and
do sympathize, and grieve with them, there is seldom much we can do to
help. Remember: It is up to you to prevent losing your hard work!

---

[5]Jeff Jeske, "Peer Editing," in *Guilford Writing Manual*, http://library.guilford.
edu/two-types-of-feedback/, accessed 11 July 2013.

Writer's Checklist for Peer Editing

_____   ✔ Does the essay stick to the topic and also deal with all the essential issues?

_____   ✔ Are the purpose—and the thesis—of the essay clear?

_____   ✔ Is evidence used effectively and documented clearly?

_____   ✔ Is the tone consistent and even handed?

_____   ✔ Are the author's views clearly evident, yet fairly presented?

_____   ✔ Is the writing clear, avoiding needless repetition?

_____   ✔ Are words used appropriately, avoiding clichés and needless verbiage?

_____   ✔ Is the essay organized clearly, so a reader can follow the argument?

_____   ✔ Do the conclusions mirror the opening in some way?

_____   ✔ What is the greatest strength of this essay?

VOICE AND STYLE

■ ■ ■

After studying this chapter, you should be able to
- Recognize and use four key modes of historical writing.
- Develop your skills of simple and direct writing.
- Take care in using word forms and punctuation.
- Modify your writing for oral presentations.

Every historian offers an individual approach to the past. Certainly the modes of expression and style of writing vary from writer to writer. Some historians are vivid and dramatic. Others are content to be more prosaic. In similar fashion, every historian develops different arguments—even when considering the same or similar topics—drawing together facts and observations to present a proposition central to an essay. Instructors will expect you to do likewise by developing a *thesis*, a main idea that unites your essay. (*Thesis* comes from a Greek word meaning "to set down.") Your thesis will be the argument, the reason you write the essay, a proposition you want others to believe. To make your argument convincing, you will need to present evidence supporting your point of view. But we should offer a fundamental caution: A mere collection of facts, specific pieces of information, is not an essay nor would it constitute an argument.

The distinguished historian Barbara Tuchman was very clear about the temptations that "facts" offer to all historians:

> To offer a mass of undigested facts, of names not identified and places not located, is of no use to the reader and is simple laziness on the part of the author, or pedantry to show how much he has read. To discard the unnecessary requires courage and also extra work...The historian is

continually being beguiled down fascinating byways and sidetracks. But the art of writing—the test of the artist—is to resist the beguilement and cleave to the subject.[1]

The facts cannot be an end in themselves. They must be carefully selected and woven together in such a way that they support a well-defined point of view you wish other people to believe. This will be the thesis of your essay, yet merely stating it clearly will be insufficient. You must also convince your readers by finding appropriate ways of writing—a writer's "voice"—that will convince them to believe the evidence you present and to accept the argument you make. In doing so, you will likely use several approaches, sometimes called modes, in your writing. The modes of writing most frequently employed by historians in supporting their arguments are *narration, description, exposition,* and *persuasion.*

MODES OF WRITING

As you study the following modes, keep in mind when writing history essays that argument, in the sense of developing a thesis, is fundamental to all the modes. You may use all of them in a single essay; certainly we have in our own writing. And although they do often overlap, the four modes of writing are distinct; one will usually predominate in a given essay or book. When you write an essay, try to determine which modes will best advance your argument. If you have a clear idea of the mode best suited to your purposes, you make the task easier for yourself and your readers.

Narration

Without narratives, history would die as a discipline. Historical narration tells us what happened, usually following the sequence of events as they happen, one event after the other. Good narrative history often looks easy to write because it is easy to read. In fact, storytelling is a complicated art. A key part of the art of narration lies in a sense of what to include and what to exclude, what to believe and what to reject. Narration must also take into

---

[1]Barbara Tuchman, "In Search of History," in *Practicing History* (New York: Ballentine Books, 1982), 18. This is actually the text of a 1963 address Tuchman gave at Radcliffe College.

account contradictions in the evidence and either resolve them or admit frankly that they cannot be resolved.

A good narrative begins by establishing some sort of tension, some kind of problem that later development of the narration should resolve. The beginning arouses readers' curiosity. It introduces elements in tension, and the rest of the story dwells on resolving or explaining that tension. Do not introduce material into your essay at the beginning if you don't intend to do something with it later on. A narration should also have a climax that embodies the meaning the writer wants readers to take from the story. At the climax, everything comes together, and the problem is solved or else explained. Because it gathers up all the threads and joins them to make the writer's point, the climax comes near the end of the essay, and your readers should feel that you have kept a promise made to them in the beginning. If you cannot find a climactic point in your narration, you need to reorganize your story. The story should move along to that point, unburdened by unnecessary details. In telling a story, it is usually better to keep quotations short and pointed, and examples limited, so that they clearly illustrate the events being recounted and readily lead to the conclusion you intend.

In the following narrative concerning the Battle of Adwa, fought in 1896 between Ethiopian forces of Emperor Menilek and Italian armies threatening to bring his country within Italy's northeastern African colonial orbit, Harold G. Marcus is spare in mentioning details and even more parsimonious in his use of quotations. He begins by indicating the plans of the Italian commander, General Oreste Baratieri, establishing an expectation of the outcome. Then he narrates the story of how the battle actually unfolded.

> The general and his army of 8,463 Italians and 10,749 Eritreans [local Africans] held the high ground between Adigrat and Idaga Hamus. Baratieri was prepared to outwit his enemy, whose limited supplies would have forced retirement southward, permitting Baratieri to claim victory and also advance deeper into Tigray....
>
> At 9:00 p.m. on 28 February, the Italians began a forced march to the three hills that dominated the Ethiopian camp, to surprise and challenge Menilek's army. To secure his left Baratieri sent his reserve brigade to an unnamed, nearby fourth hill, but the Ethiopian guide, either through misdirection or sabotage, led the Italians astray. Not only was the left flank uncovered but also a quarter of the Italian force was rendered useless and vulnerable. So, even if Baratieri's army had occupied the high points and deployed in strong defensive positions on the frontal slopes, it was foredoomed to defeat. Indeed, the timing of the Italian attack, as a surprise on early Sunday morning, was all wrong.

At 4:00 a.m., on 1 March, Menilek, |Empress| Taitou, and the rases |chief political and military subordinates of the Emperor| were at mass, which the Orthodox church celebrates early. It was a sad time, since the food situation had forced the emperor to order camp to be struck on 2 March. His relief must have been great when a number of couriers and runners rushed in to report the enemy was approaching in force. The emperor ordered men to arms, and, as the soldiers lined up, priests passed before them hearing confession, granting absolution, and offering blessings. The green, orange, and red flags of Ethiopia were unfurled when the emperor appeared, and the soldiers cheered and cheered. At 5:30 a.m., Menilek's 100,000-man army moved forward, to confront an Italian force of 14,500 soldiers.

By 9:00 a.m., the outcome was obvious. The Italian center had crumbled, and other units were in danger of being flanked by Ethiopians who had found the gap in Baratieri's defenses. By noon, when retreat sounded, the Italians had paid dearly. Four thousand Europeans and 2,000 Eritreans had died, 1,428 of Baratieri's soldiers had been wounded, and 1,800 prisoners were held by the Ethiopians. All told, the Italian army lost 70 percent of its forces, a disaster for a modern army.

In sharp contrast, Menilek's forces suffered an estimated 4,000–7,000 killed and perhaps as many as 10,000 wounded, which made for an acceptably low loss ratio. The Italian enemy had been destroyed, whereas the Ethiopian army remained in being, strengthened by the weapons and matériel abandoned on the field. The victory was unequivocally Ethiopian.

In telling the story of this imperial encounter, Marcus poses a problem and then narrates the story to its unexpected conclusion. Although many other sources are available concerning the conflict at Adwa, including Italian official records, letters and diaries of soldiers, not to mention oral testimonies collected from some of the participants, Marcus wisely elects not to infuse his narration with too much of this potentially extraneous information. He uses just enough evidence—primarily the numbers of soldiers engaged in the battle and the numbers of casualties—in a way that lends credibility to his account. And thus you are disposed to believe him when he later goes on to conclude that Menilek's victory at the Battle of Adwa did "guarantee Ethiopia another generation and one-half of virtually unchallenged independence; it gave the country a status similar to that of Afghanistan, Persia, Japan, and Thailand as accepted anomalies in the imperialist world order."[2] And you can see how his narration of this battle experience supports the essential argument he makes in his book.

---

[2]Harold G. Marcus, *A History of Ethiopia*, updated ed. (Berkeley: University of California Press, 2002), 98–100.

Of course, in your research you might just as well consult some of the numerous published (and perhaps, if your college or university has its own archive, also unpublished) collections of letters, as well as journals and collected papers. They offer similar opportunities for research enabling you to write narrations of other stories concerning the past. Not just battles, but also the lives of individuals, and even the explanations they offer for the circumstances of their existence, can become fascinating subjects for your history essays.

Description

As straightforward as narration may sometimes appear, description presents an account of sensory experience—the way things look, feel, taste, sound, and smell—as well as more impressionistic descriptions of attitudes and behavior. Popular history includes vivid descriptions, and you, too, can describe people and places with great effect in an essay intended for a college or scholarly audience. No matter how learned or unlearned in the limitless facts of a historical period, everyone has had sensory experiences similar to, if not exactly the same as, those of people in the past. Therefore, description is useful to kindle the imagination of readers and draw them into the story you wish to tell. Jonathon Spence does exactly that as he begins his study of life in seventeenth-century provincial China, *The Death of Woman Wang*.

> The earthquake struck T'an-ch'eng on July 25, 1668. It was evening, the moon just rising. There was no warning, save for a frightening roar that seemed to come from somewhere to the northwest. The buildings in the city began to shake and the trees took up a rhythmical swaying, tossing ever more wildly back and forth until their tips almost touched the ground. Then came one sharp violent jolt that brought down stretches of the city walls and battlements, officials' yamens [or residences], temples, and thousands of private homes. Broad fissures opened up across the streets and underneath the houses. Jets of water spurted into the air to a height of twenty feet or more, and streams of water poured down the roads and flooded the irrigation ditches. Those who tried to remain standing felt as if their feet were round stones spinning out of control and were brought crashing to the ground....
>
> As suddenly as it had come the earthquake departed. The ground was still. The water seeped away, leaving the open fissures edged with mud and fine sand. The ruins rested in layers where they had fallen, like giant sets of steps.[3]

---

[3]Jonathon D. Spence, *The Death of Woman Wang* (New York: Viking Press, 1978), 1–2.

All these descriptions of the earthquake will resonate with any reader who has likewise lived through such an experience and also with those who understand earthquakes only from seeing images of them and their aftermath on television. The vivid descriptions will make it easy for you to imagine being transported to eastern China more than three centuries ago. And by introducing his study with such clear and believable descriptions, Professor Spence has prepared you to trust his analysis of life in a society that is likely far different from any of your experiences. You can often accomplish much the same effect in your essays by careful attention to description. But never make things up when you describe something. Although some readers may be entertained by flights of fancy in historical writing, historians find them cheap and dishonest, and with good reason.

Exposition

Rather than providing details of events or sensory experience, expositions explain and analyze—philosophical ideas, causes of events, the significance of decisions, the motives of participants, the working of an organization, the ideology of a political party. Any time you set out to explain cause and effect, or the meaning of an event or an idea, you write in the expository mode. Of course, exposition may coexist in an essay with other modes of writing. The narrator who tells *what* happened usually devotes some paragraphs to telling *why* it happened—and so goes into expository writing. Some historical essays are fairly evenly balanced between narrative and exposition, telling both what happened and why, explaining the significance of the story. Many historical essays are primarily expositions, especially those that break down and analyze a text or event to tell readers what it means—even as the author narrates what happened that makes the explanation necessary.

One important category of expository writing, especially in college courses, is the historiographic essay. These "histories of histories," as they are sometimes called, can be very important in helping students understand the evidence and arguments historians have used when considering a particular topic or some corollary of it. Students are often asked to write such essays, though we have found that many of our students frequently find such an exercise very difficult. Perhaps this is because they prefer to stick to the facts, and treating ideas themselves as facts in such an essay sometimes seems overwhelming. But you should not be fearful of such an effort. If you approach it as simply another form of historical analysis, it won't be as difficult as you may at first imagine.

There are many examples of historiographic essays in a wide variety of historical journals; you would do well to look for them and familiarize yourself with this common form of historical writing. Many contain detailed analyses, which cannot be usefully illustrated in a short excerpt, but this selection from an essay by David Brion Davis will give you some idea of how to approach a historiographic exposition:

> During the past thirty years, our understanding of American slavery has been extraordinarily enriched by numerous studies that fall in the... category of rigorous and sustained comparison. One thinks particularly of the work of Carl Degler comparing slavery and race relations in Brazil and the United States; George M. Fredrickson's two volumes on white supremacy and its consequences in the United States and South Africa; and Peter Kolchin's comparison and analysis of American slavery and Russian serfdom, a project that greatly broadened and enriched his subsequent survey of American slavery from 1619 to 1877. Mention should also be made of more specialized studies, such as those by Shearer Davis Bowman on U.S. planters and Prussian Junkers, by Eugene D. Genovese and Michael Craton on slave rebellions, and by Richard S. Dunn on two specific plantations in Virginia and Jamaica. While the comparative method *can* lead to mechanical listings of similarities and differences, it would clearly be useful to have more comparative studies on such specific subjects as domestic servants, slave artisans, and slaves in urban and manufacturing jobs. Peter Kolchin has candidly pointed to the severe problems comparative history faces, problems that help to explain the somewhat limited number of such full-length studies; yet I think that the cumulative benefit of comparative work can be seen in the global awareness of historians such as Thomas Holt, when writing on Jamaica; Rebecca Scott, when writing on Brazil and Cuba; Frederick Cooper, when writing on East Africa; and Seymour Drescher, when writing on British abolitionism and other subjects—to say nothing of the omnipresent economic historian Stanley L. Engerman, whose work on various forms of unfree labor could hardly be broader in perspective.
>
> But while careful, empirical comparison is indispensable, especially in alerting us to the importance of such matters as the demography and sex ratios of slave societies, the differences in slave communities, and the social implications of resident as opposed to absentee

planters, much recent research has also underscored the importance of "the Big Picture"—the interrelationships that constituted an Atlantic Slave System as well as the place of such racial slavery in the evolution of the Western and modern worlds.[4]

Of course, Davis brings the experience of a distinguished career in writing about slavery to his historiographic exposition. Yet the works he mentions would be easily accessible to a student searching for histories written on the subject of slavery, and the categories he uses to group the studies would be readily observable to anyone who read them carefully. Professor Davis continues with consideration of numerous other works on the subject of his essay, "Slavery from Broader Perspectives," but he might just as well have analyzed and compared the arguments in the more than twenty books and articles he mentions. The latter effort would, as well, have resulted in a thoughtful historiographic essay, and one within the scope of many undergraduates of our acquaintance. By applying your mind to careful research, thoughtful reading, and careful analysis, you could also create a similarly substantial exposition about how historians have, over time, written about slavery—or almost any other serious subject.

Persuasion

In addition to presenting details and analysis, historians also use persuasion in their writing to take a position on a subject; such essays are most interesting when the topics are important and the evidence is open to interpretation. On any important historical issue, you will find disagreement among historians. These disagreements are valuable in that they discourage becoming frozen in an intolerance of opposition, and debates may actually encourage toleration in the present. The disagreements also help readers see the sources in a different light. Such disagreements thrive in book reviews. A historian who disagrees with another may make a counterargument to a book the reviewer thinks is incorrect. Jacob Burckhardt's *Civilization of the Renaissance in Italy*, published in 1860, has provoked a virtual library of responses: reviews, articles, and even books attempting to

---

[4]David Brion Davis, "*AHR Forum:* Looking at Slavery from Broader Perspectives," *The American Historical Review* 105 (2000): 453–454; we have eliminated Professor Davis's footnotes, which include complete citations to the many works he mentions.

persuade readers that Burckhardt was right or wrong in his interpretation of the Renaissance—or arguing that he was partly right and partly wrong. Frederick Jackson Turner's thesis concerning the role of the frontier in U.S. history has been similarly provocative.

Of course, when you set out the thesis for your essay, you will also be using persuasion in an effort to convince readers to accept your central argument. Always state your thesis concisely and as early as possible in your essay, followed by an indication of the main points and evidence you will use in making your case. When you make an assertion essential in your efforts to persuade readers, always provide some examples as evidence. A general statement followed by a quotation or some other concrete reference to the evidence provides readers reason to believe you. In this example about volunteer nursing by French women during World War I, historian Margaret H. Darrow seeks to persuade readers to accept what at first seems to be a paradox. The myths of war held that it was "full of honor, courage, heroism, self-sacrifice, and manliness." Nurses treating the wounded and the dying were caught not only by the power of the myth but also by the reality of what they saw; they had a hard time reconciling the two. Darrow offers this observation on the problem:

> Few memoirs resolved the tension between the rhetoric of noble suffering and heroic sacrifice and the reality of dirt, pain, fear, and fatigue, with most memoirs swinging from one mode to the other without any attempt at reconciliation. For example, Noëlle Roger began her description of a ward of seriously wounded soldiers with the claim that "each of these men had lived a glorious adventure." She then depicted the shrieking pain of a man brought from the operating table, the rigid terror of a tetanus victim, and the hallucinations of a shell-shock case. However, her intent was not irony; she did not seem to notice—or could not express—that none of these were glorious adventures.[5]

Here is a standard pattern in historical writing—follow it whenever you can. Professor Darrow first makes a general statement; then she offers a quotation and a summary of the evidence. A reader will more likely be persuaded by the argument because she has provided specific evidence for it. You can do likewise in your essays.

You will be more persuasive if you admit any weakness in your argument. If you admit the places where your argument is weak and consider

---

[5]Margaret H. Darrow, "French Volunteer Nursing and the Myth of War Experience in World War I," *The American Historical Review* 101 (1996): 100.

counterarguments fairly, giving your reasons for rejecting them, you will build confidence in your judgments among readers. You may concede that some evidence stands against your proposition. But you may then explain that this evidence is not as important or as trustworthy as the evidence you adduce for your point of view. Or you may argue that the contrary evidence has been misinterpreted. But always stay on the subject of your argument throughout your essay. Inexperienced writers sometimes try to throw everything they know into an essay as if it were a soup and the more ingredients the better. Take the advice of Barbara Tuchman offered at the beginning of this chapter and resist "being beguiled down fascinating byways and sidetracks" only marginally related to your topic. Get to your point. Trust your readers. Moreover, trust yourself. Do as much as you can in as few words as possible. Your essays will be more persuasive if you do!

SIMPLE AND DIRECT WRITING

Thinking about these four modes of expression as you begin will help you clarify your writing task. You can then define more precisely your reason for writing an essay, plan your research, and organize what you will write. Having these in mind will also help you in giving voice to your ideas and improving the style of what you write. We have appreciated the advice about writing summarized in the title of a book on the subject—*Simple and Direct*—by the respected American historian, Jacques Barzun. Of course, it is not always that simple. Among historians, writing conventions—which are neither laws nor strict rules, but rather simply customary practices—are important. If you depart from the conventions, you run the risk of not being taken seriously.

In seeking your writing voice, and in striving for a consistent style, you may be tempted to follow the all too common advice to "write as we speak. That is absurd," as Barzun plainly writes:

> Most speaking is not plain or direct, but vague, clumsy, confused, and wordy. This last fault appears in every transcript from taped conversation, which is why we say *"reduce to writing."* What is meant by the advice to write as we speak is to write *as we might* speak if we spoke extremely well. This means that good writing should not sound stuffy, pompous, highfalutin, totally unlike ourselves, but rather, well—"simple & direct."[6]

---

[6]Jacques Barzun, *Simple & Direct: A Rhetoric for Writers* (New York: Harper & Row, 1975), 12–13. Emphasis in original.

You will be better able to reach this goal as you revise your essay. In addition to the sensible advice that you read your essay carefully— even reading it aloud to be sure you have written what you intended— there are several key areas to keep in mind as you prepare even the first draft. Following these basic writing conventions will help you develop a distinctive voice and personal writing style, which will serve you, and your readers, well.

Write in Coherent Paragraphs

Paragraphs are groups of sentences bound together by a controlling idea and intended to help readability. Indentations break the monotony of long columns of type. They help readers follow the text with greater ease, signaling a slight change in subject from what has gone before, and announce that the paragraph to follow will develop a thought that can usually be summarized in a simple statement. A good rule of thumb is to have one or two paragraph indentations on every typed manuscript page. It is only a rule of thumb—not a command. And for historical writing it is also a good idea to avoid the one- or two-sentence paragraphs common in journalism.

All paragraphs are built on the first sentence, and the following sentences in the paragraph should run in a natural flow from it. Although the paragraph is a flexible form, most readable paragraphs depend on connectors, sometimes a word in one sentence that is repeated in the next. The connectors tie your sentences together—and therefore link your thoughts. You can often test paragraph coherence by seeing if every sentence has connectors that join its thought in some way to the previous sentence all the way back to the first sentence in the paragraph. Similar patterns of repetition hold all prose together. Each sentence both repeats something from previous sentences—a word, a synonym, or an idea—while adding something new to the information readers already possess.

Even in this short paragraph by Robert C. Post you can see a pattern of connectors at work:

> New Yorkers always had a keen appreciation for transportation innova-
> tions, and in fact the first locomotive built in the United States came
> from the West Point Foundry in New York City. But New Yorkers had just
> celebrated the opening of the Erie Canal, tapping a western hinterland.
> Thus, enthusiasm for railways was strongest in cities which had not yet
> done so with their own hinterland, including Boston, Charleston, and

particularly Baltimore, the third largest city in the country with a population nearing 80,000. For none of these cities did a canal like the Erie appear to be a viable option. A railroad was.[7]

Look for similar connectors in the paragraphs of historical accounts as you read, and think about them when you write. Doing so will help you develop greater coherence to your thought, and you can develop a feel for what should be in a paragraph and what should not.

Keep Sentences Manageable

Your sentences, too, should always focus on the most important idea you want to convey in that statement. Try not to entangle your sentences with other information you cannot readily develop or that is not related directly to some previous information in your essay. One way to keep sentences manageable is to avoid multiplying dependent clauses, which act as adjectives or adverbs and modify other elements in a sentence. We do not want to suggest you should avoid dependent clauses altogether, rather that you should not make them so numerous they cause you to lose control of your sentences and make your prose difficult to read. You will help keep your thinking clear if in writing sentences you think first of the subject, then of what you want to say about it. It seldom improves your writing to bury your real subject in a dependent clause. Indeed, most readable writers use dependent clauses only once or twice in every three or four sentences.

Here is a fine, readable paragraph by historians Oscar and Lilian Handlin, from their book, *Liberty in Expansion;* note the close relation between subjects and verbs in the sentences—even in the dependent clauses.

> The healing image meant much to a government, not all of whose statesmen were pure of heart and noble of impulse. On January 30, 1798, the House of Representatives being in session in Philadelphia, Mr. Rufus Griswold of Connecticut alluded to a story that Mr. Matthew Lyon of Vermont had been forced to wear a wooden sword for cowardice in the field. Thereupon Mr. Lyon spat in Mr. Griswold's face. Sometime later, Mr. Griswold went to Macalister's store on Chestnut Street and bought the biggest hickory stick available. He proceeded to the House, where, in the presence of the whole

---

[7]Robert C. Post, *Technology, Transport, and Travel in American History* (Washington, DC: American Historical Association, 2003), 44; we have deleted source citations.

Congress and with Mr. Speaker urging him on, he beat Mr. Lyon about the head and shoulders. An effort to censure both actors in the drama failed.[8]

Making sure you connect the subjects of your sentences closely to the verbs that describe the actions they are taking—and that you use singular subjects with singular verbs, and plural subjects with plural verbs—will also help you focus on another important stylistic element of good writing.

Avoid the Passive Voice

Writing in the passive voice may seem more comfortable and less aggressive, but it removes the directness of your words. Use the active voice, instead; it's not only more direct, but it generally makes what you want to say clearer to your readers. In sentences using the active voice, the subject is the focus of the sentence taking the action, as in this sentence in the active voice:

> ```
> President John F. Kennedy made the decision to
> invade Cuba.
> ```

However, in sentences using the passive voice, the action itself is the most important thing, often obscuring who took the action, as in this sentence on the same subject:

> ```
> The decision was made to invade Cuba.
> ```

In the passive voice we do not know who made the decision unless we add the clumsy prepositional phrase *by President John F. Kennedy* at the end. Leaving off that last phrase would eliminate an essential part of the information for your readers, but adding it at the end makes the president's action see almost an afterthought.

Readable historians use the passive only when they have a reason for doing so. Use the passive when the obvious importance of the sentence is that the subject is acted upon:

> ```
> Bill Clinton was elected to a second term as
> president of the United States in November 1996.
> ```

The passive may also help keep the focus of a paragraph on a person or group where the agent is understood throughout. In the following

---

[8]Oscar and Lilian Handlin, *Liberty in Expansion: 1760-1850* (New York: Harper & Row, 1989), 160.

paragraph from a history of the Russian Revolution of 1917 and afterward, the passive voice is used several times. We have indicated clauses using the passive in italics. Study them to understand how the author, Orlando Figes, uses the passive voice:

> The Kronstadt Naval Base, an island of sailor-militants in the Gulf of Finland just off Petrograd, was by far the most rebellious stronghold of this Bolshevik vanguard. The sailors were young trainees who had seen very little military activity during the war. They had spent the previous year cooped up on board their ships with their officers, who treated them with more than the usual sadistic brutality since the normal rules of naval discipline did not apply to trainees. Each ship was a tinderbox of hatred and violence. During the February Days the sailors mutinied with awesome ferocity. *Admiral Viren, the Base Commander, was hacked to death with bayonets, and dozens of other officers were murdered, lynched or imprisoned in the island dungeons. The old naval hierarchy was completely destroyed* and effective power passed to the Kronstadt Soviet. It was an October in February. *The authority of the Provisional Government was never really established, nor was military order restored.* Kerensky, the Minister of Justice, proved utterly powerless in his repeated efforts to gain jurisdiction over the imprisoned officers, *despite rumours in the bourgeois press that they had been brutally tortured.*[9]

The focus of the paragraph is the consequence of the uprising of the sailors at Kronstadt. Thus, in this paragraph, the passive voice helps keep that focus.

Our best advice is this: When you use the passive voice, ask yourself *why* you are doing so. If you do not have a clear reason for the passive, rewrite your sentence using the active voice.

Write About the Past in the Past Tense

Inexperienced writers also sometimes strive for dramatic effect by shifting their prose into the historical present. They may write something like this:

```
    The issue as Calvin Coolidge sees it is
this: The government has been intervening too
much in private affairs. He is now the head of
the government. He will do as little as possible.
He keeps silent when people ask him favors. He
```

---

[9]Orlando Figes, *A People's Tragedy: A History of the Russian Revolution* (New York: Viking, 1997), 394–395.

> says things like this: "The chief business of the
> American people is business." He does not believe
> the government should intervene in the business
> process. Within a year after Coolidge leaves
> office, the Great Depression begins.

Such an effort is usually intended to provide life to the drama of history, to make it seem that it is all happening again as we read. But the effort is frequently counterproductive; overuse of the present tense can become tedious after a while and is often confusing. In American, as well as British, historical convention, it is most appropriate to use the past tense to write about the past. It is, however, permissible to use the present tense in describing a piece of writing (even the transcript of a speech) or a work of art because such works are assumed always to be present to the person who reads, hears, or observes them.

However, you may often do better using the past tense. This is especially true when you do not intend to give an extended summary of the work, as in this example:

> In his "Cross of Gold" speech delivered at the
> Democratic National Convention in 1896, William
> Jennings Bryan took the side of the impoverished
> farmers who thought that inflation would help raise
> the prices they received for their crops.

In this case, the emphasis is on Bryan rather than on the speech itself; thus the simple past tense seems more appropriate. Again, keeping the focus on what is most important in your writing is your best guide.

Sometimes our students copy a similar pattern from what they hear on television, and in particular from sportscasters who have adopted dramatic phrasing in an attempt to make their reports more exciting. The football play-by-play announcer who describes a touchdown run ("he could go all the way!") seems to have influenced the misuse of conditional statements concerning the past in too many student essays. Much better simply to use the past tense in the historical stories you write. You will help readers most when writing about the past by using the past tense in your essays.

Connect Your First and Last Paragraphs

You will also help your readers keep the central message of your essay clear in their minds if you make sure the first and last paragraphs have some obvious relationship. In most published writing—for example, the first and last paragraphs of an article or chapters in a book—have such coherence. You can read them without reading the intervening material and have at least a fairly good idea of what comes between. Now and then you will find a piece of writing where the first and last paragraphs do not have a clear connection. But writers wishing to be sure that their work holds together can help their efforts by seeing to it that each essay ends in a paragraph that reflects some words and thoughts appearing in the first. Notice how Penny Sonnenburg's essay in Appendix A is constructed in this way. Turn through the pages of *The American Historical Review* or the *Journal of World History,* or even popular journals of opinion such as *The Atlantic* or *The New Yorker,* and you will see that first and last paragraphs mirror each other in most of the essays.

WORD FORMS AND PUNCTUATION

Careful attention as you read historical works will also provide examples of the judicious use of words and punctuation. And it should be readily apparent, as we noted at the beginning of this chapter, that simple and direct writing is more difficult than ordinary speaking. Sometimes in the physical labor of writing, our minds wander, and we make errors using words and punctuation. That is, we violate conventions. Most people can spot such errors by reading their work carefully aloud. You can usually trust your ear. When something does not sound right, try changing it. Having someone else read what you have written can also be invaluable, whether informally at your invitation or as part of a peer editing process. We would also encourage you to seek advice, not least from your instructor. For many years, American college students also have benefited from the suggestions of William Strunk and E. B. White in *The Elements of Style;* we especially recommend to you the recently available fiftieth anniversary edition.[10] But the following suggestions about a few common writing difficulties will provide a start as you seek to improve your writing and develop a readable style and voice for your essays.

Keep Modifiers Under Control

Adjectives modify nouns, while adverbs modify verbs, adjectives, and other adverbs. Both adjectives and adverbs can sometimes weaken the concept of the words they modify. However, a good adjective or adverb, when

---

[10]William Strunk and E. B. White, *The Elements of Style,* 50th anniversary ed. (New York: Longman, 2008).

well used in a necessary place, can brighten a sentence. Our best advice is to use both sparingly. The proportion of one adjective to every twelve or thirteen words is fairly constant among published writers in America. The proportion of adverbs to other words is somewhat less. Of course, these proportions are not absolute; for some purposes you may have to use more. But be sure you need the adjectives and adverbs you use.

You may also use descriptive participial phrases, often to open sentences. But you must be sure they modify the subject you intend; otherwise, you run the risk of making your prose incomprehensible and perhaps even ridiculous to readers. For example, consider this sentence:

> Living in a much less violent society, the idea that every man, woman, and child in the United States has a right to his or her very own assault rifle seems ridiculous to most Canadians.

Who or what lives in that less violent society? The idea? The sentence is much clearer if rewritten like this:

> Living in a much less violent society, Canadians find ridiculous the idea that every man, woman, and child in the United States has the right to his or her very own assault rifle.

Keep such qualifying phrases close to the words they are intended to modify, just as you would when using adjectives and adverbs.

Be Certain Pronouns Refer to Antecedents

Pronouns stand for nouns that are said to be the *antecedent* of the pronoun. Definite pronouns, such as *he, she, it, him, her, they, them,* and *their,* stand for nouns that usually appear somewhere before them in a sentence or paragraph. Be sure to make the pronoun reference clear even if you must revise the sentence considerably. You will confuse readers if you write:

> The Czechs disdained the Slovaks because they were more cosmopolitan.

To whom does the pronoun *they* refer? Were the Czechs or the Slovaks more cosmopolitan? You would do better to rewrite the sentence, like this:

> The more cosmopolitan Czechs disdained the more rural Slovaks.

While the original may be perfectly clear to *you,* your readers will much appreciate the revised version.

Form Plurals and Possessives of Nouns Accurately

Be sure to note differences between plurals and collective nouns. For example, the singular is *peasant,* the plural is *peasants,* but the collective class in European history is called the *peasantry.* We may call a man or woman who works in a factory a *proletarian,* and a group of them on an assembly line might be called by Marxists *proletarians.* But Marx called the whole class the *proletariat.* We may speak of a *noble* or an *aristocrat* when we speak of the highest social ranks in some societies, and a group of such people would be called *nobles* or *aristocrats,* but the whole class is called the *nobility* or the *aristocracy.*

Take care not to use an apostrophe to form a plural. Do not write,

```
The Wilsons' went to Washington.
```

The correct form is

```
The Wilsons went to Washington.
```

The plurals of dates and acronyms do not use the apostrophe. So you should write about the 1960s or the NCOs (noncommissioned officers such as sergeants) in the armed forces.

The apostrophe is used for the possessive, showing ownership or a particular relation. Some writers and editors add only an apostrophe to singular nouns ending in *s.* But we believe the better, and more easily understood, practice is to make the possessive of these words as you would do others, like this:

```
Erasmus's works
Chambers's book
```

For plural nouns that end in *s,* add just an apostrophe to form the possessive:

```
the Germans' plan
the neighbors' opinions
```

For plurals that do not end in *s,* form the possessive as you would for singular nouns:

```
women's history
children's rights
```

Use Intended Forms for Common Words

The contraction *it's* stands for *it is* or, sometimes, *it has*. But the possessive pronoun *its* means "belonging to it." Here are some examples:

> `It's` almost impossible to guarantee safe travel.
>
> `It's` been hard to measure the effects on the country.
>
> The idea had lost `its` power before 1900.

Similarly, you should distinguish appropriately between the contraction *you're*, which stands for *you are*, the possessive *your*, and the noun *yore* occasionally used to describe the past. Each of these should be used as in the following examples:

> `You're` going to the picnic, aren't you?
>
> Will you take `your` umbrella?
>
> We'll have a good time, just as we did in days of `yore`.

You will recognize that these distinctions are ones your word processor's spell checking program will not recognize, so they require you to be especially diligent in proofreading. Similar confusions abound with the words *site*—as in *Web site* or *historic site*—and *sight*, which describes what we do with our eyes; the verb *cite* can also cause confusion with these, especially since it is coming into unfortunate use as a noun in place of a *citation* you would make to document your sources. Perhaps the most common such error we see in student essays is the accidental confusion between plural possessive *their* and the noun or adverb *there*, specifying a particular place, and occasionally the contraction *they're* (for *they are*). Pay careful attention to these differences! Your failure to do so will often mark your essay as particularly careless.

Use Objective Case Pronouns Appropriately

The nominative or subjective forms of pronouns include *I, we, he, she, who, they,* and *those*. The objective forms include versions such as *me, us, him, her, whom,* and *them*. The nominative is used as the subject of a sentence or a clause:

> I read Huizinga's books.
>
> The Prince said `he` was not the king's son.

The objective should be used for the object of a preposition:

> It was a matter between *him* and *me*.
> Between *you* and *me*, I made a mistake.

And the objective should be used in an indirect object:

> The president gave *her* a cabinet position.

Objective forms should be used as the subject or an object of an infinitive verb. The infinitive is the verb form that includes the infinitive marker *to* and the dictionary form of the verb. Thus *to go, to be, to dwell,* and *to see* are all infinitives. The subject of the infinitive is a noun or pronoun that comes before the infinitive in a sentence, that does the action the infinitive expresses:

> King Leopold wanted *him* to go at once to Africa.

In the preceding example, the person designated by the objective pronoun *him* will go to Africa. Since he will do the going—the action expressed in the infinitive *to go*—the pronoun *him* is the subject of the infinitive and is in the objective case.

Maintain Parallel Form for a Series

English and American writers often use words or phrases in a series, but the units in the series must stand as grammatical equals. Therefore, you should *not* write sentences like this:

> Richelieu wanted three things for France—
> authority for the king, an end to religious strife,
> and he also wanted secure "natural" frontiers.

This series begins with nouns modified by prepositional phrases, but the last element is a clause. The sentence should be rewritten something like this:

> Richelieu wanted three things for France—
> authority for the king, an end to religious strife,
> and secure "natural" frontiers.

Similar attention to the details of your writing applies to matters of punctuation and will likewise help readers understand the intentions of your essays.

Use Commas and Semicolons Appropriately

Independent clauses—which could stand alone as sentences—can be separated from one another by commas, but only when you use linking words. Without the linking words, you should use semicolons. Do not join independent clauses with commas alone. Study these appropriate examples:

> The McNary-Haugen bill would have provided subsidies for American farmers, but President Coolidge vetoed it in 1927.
>
> The people of the United States decided that they must give up Prohibition; the law brought about too many social disruptions.

You should, however, use commas to set off long introductory phrases:

> Even after the transcontinental railroad was completed in 1867, some pioneers still made the trip West by covered wagon.

Also use commas to separate items—whether words or phrases—in a series:

> President Franklin D. Roosevelt moved to solve problems of unemployment, banking, and despair.
>
> William Jennings Bryan campaigned for the presidency in 1896 by traveling 18,000 miles, making 600 speeches, and attacking the "moneyed interests."

However, if the series follows a colon, the items should be separated by semicolons:

> William Jennings Bryan campaigned for the presidency in 1896, while insisting on several key positions: attacking bankers, whom he called

```
the "moneyed interests"; supporting farmers; and
promoting the silver standard.
```

Similarly, you can use commas to set off nonrestrictive words and phrases, when you can substitute the word *and* for the comma and still have a sensible sentence:

```
    Ralph Waldo Emerson was a tall, frail, and
elegant man.
```

In this case you could write instead, "Ralph Waldo Emerson was a tall and frail and elegant man." But do not use commas between adjectives where you cannot sensibly replace the comma with *and*. You can write:

```
The three old maple trees stood on the hill.
```

But you *cannot* write:

```
The three and old and maple trees stood on the
hill.
```

Carefully Present and Punctuate Quotations

When you use quotations in your essays, you should take special care in using punctuation, as well as lowercase and capital letters. If the quotation is to blend into the text of your essay, change lowercase and capital letters, as well as punctuation, so that the quotation will fit into your own sentence.

```
    Kipling urged Americans "to take up the White
Man's burden."
```

You do not need to use brackets to indicate you have made such changes. Nor should you use ellipsis marks (three dots, like this...; some word processing programs may insert them automatically, without spaces, like this...) at the beginning or end of the quotation. The quotation marks alone indicate you are beginning or ending your quotation at that point. However, you *should* use ellipsis marks to indicate any words you have left out in the middle of a quotation; but if the deleted material includes a period, you should use four ellipsis marks.

Commas and periods, no matter whether they were in the original or you insert them as a part of your own sentences using quotations, should go *inside* the quotation marks. This will make what you write clearer to readers. However, a question mark at the end of a quotation goes within the final quotation marks *only* if the quotation itself is a question. If you are using the quotation as part of a question you wish to pose, then the question mark should go outside the quotation marks. The same is true of exclamations. Semicolons and colons always go outside the final quotation marks, no matter if they were in the original quotation or not.

Any quotation longer than four or five lines in your essay should be indented five spaces and set up as a block within your text. Double-space such block quotations, and do not enclose them with quotation marks. The only quotation marks you should use with block quotations are those that appear within the original source you are quoting. Your instructor may want you to put block quotations in single-spaced text as your essays usually will not be for publication. Since it is difficult to edit single-spaced text, you would, however, always double-space any material intended for publication. The quotations we have used from the works of other historians in this book should serve as models of how you can use quotations from your sources in your own essays.

THE FINAL PRESENTATION

No matter how diligent you are in developing an appropriate writing voice and finding a consistent style, the appearance of your essay—in either an electronic or print version—tells readers many things about you as a writer. A slovenly, scarcely readable version signals a writer who cares little for the subject or for readers. As a writer you may care deeply; make sure your readers can see this from the final version you present to them. Computers make things easier for writers and readers alike, and most writers and students nowadays use computers with word processing programs. Take advantage of the capabilities of the computer and create a clean copy of your essay.

Using your word processing program, take special care to eliminate typographical errors, misspellings, words left out or duplicated, and other such mistakes. Also number the pages of your essay, even if it will be submitted only in an electronic version. Every word processing program will allow you to do so; figure out the steps your program uses to number pages, and use them to insert page numbers into your essay. Your instructor may give you other specific directions about formatting your essay. Follow them. Lacking instructions, you usually will not go wrong if you follow the format of the model research paper in Appendix A of this book. Once you have completed these final corrections and formatting, you can save the final version of your essay—making sure to keep several copies, not all of them saved on your computer alone!

If a printed version of your essay is required, once you have saved the electronic file, you can finally print a clean copy. Again, follow any instructions you have been given, but if you have none, here are some suggestions. Use a good quality 8 1/2 × 11-inch white bond paper. Double-space the essay and print it on one side of the page only. Leave margins wide enough for comments your instructor may wish to make, no less than one inch on the top, bottom, and each side. Use Times New Roman, Bookman Old Style, Courier, or some other clean, easy-to-read type font and be sure the ink from the printer is dark enough to be read easily. If you must, and if your instructor will accept a handwritten essay, use lined white paper and write in dark blue or black ink on every line. Use a cover page giving your name, the name of your instructor, the name of your course, and the time your class meets. Fasten the pages of your essay with a paper clip or with a staple in the upper left-hand corner. Binders, however, are almost always a nuisance to an instructor, adding bulk and making it awkward to write comments in the margins. It seldom is helpful to use them.

The presentation of your essay—as an electronic file or a printed paper—is the last place where your adherence to historians' conventions is evident. But it is the first impression your instructor will have of your essay! Take advantage of that opportunity. But remember, if you ignore the conventions, you may discover that the grade you receive may be less than you otherwise desire.

WRITING FOR SPEAKING

Sometimes you will be expected to present your research in an oral presentation. Historians often refer to this as "reading a paper"; we have often done this at academic conferences or in lecture presentations. But what you *read* is not exactly the same as what you write in a formal essay. So on occasion you may need to modify your writing to make your oral presentations as clear and fluid as they can be. This might be the only writing you will do for an assignment, but more often you will need to write your essay first and then create another version for an oral presentation.

A first consideration should be length. How long will you be expected to speak? Allow about one page (usually 250 words) for each two minutes you will need to talk. But try reading something you have written first to be sure that you can read clearly at such a pace. You might need to adjust the length of your essay to better match the pace of your speech. Also keep in mind that for this task, the dictum—"simple and direct"—which we mentioned earlier, is especially important. But when writing something that you will read, be constantly aware that what you write needs to make it possible for you to speak extremely well. When confronting this problem, one of us was reminded by an old radio newscaster that a semicolon has no sound! That was above all a reminder that in writing for speaking, simple and direct sentences are best. Any nuances of meaning you might be tempted to include in a complex sentence will, when read, most likely be lost on listeners.

Also keep in mind the entire audience you will have. While you may write an essay specifically for an instructor, there almost certainly will be others listening to your presentation. If you can captivate all, or at least most, of your listeners, you will also capture the attention of your instructor or whoever will be evaluating your presentation. Try not to use very many quotations, and make those that you do include brief and to the point. And there is really no way to make citations to your sources as you speak. Just like semicolons, footnotes do not translate well into the spoken word. You might better try to write a brief section, maybe just two or three sentences, discussing the research that has led to your main points. Perhaps a single example will also be sufficient where you might have offered several in a formal essay. Work to keep your listeners focused on your main points rather than attempting to navigate a field of details.

Finally, remember that writing the text is not the end of your preparation for making a presentation. You will still need to be certain about how you will read the essay and what the circumstances will be. Above all, practice reading what you have written. Have a friend listen to you do so at least once. Plan on making pauses so that you can take a breath. Thomas Jefferson marked places in what he had written—even the Declaration of Independence—where he could easily breathe so that his presentations would be more readily understood. Try doing so for your oral report!

Also make sure you know where you will be talking. Even if it is a familiar classroom, if at all possible actually go to the room beforehand and stand where you will be expected to make your presentation. Get the potential distractions in your mind. And be sure you know about anything you might need, such as a high table or lectern; if you need one, or any other equipment for your presentation, be sure to ask in advance. As you prepare for making an oral presentation, you may also find especially helpful the suggestions offered by Professor Linda Kerber, former president of the American Historical Association, in her article "Conference Rules."[11]

Writer's Checklist for Expression and Conventions

_____ ✔ What must I include in my narrative? What might I leave out?

_____ ✔ Have I based my descriptions on sound evidence?

_____ ✔ Do the descriptions bring sensory experience to mind?

_____ ✔ Are my inferences credible and clearly explained?

_____ ✔ Have I argued persuasively?

_____ ✔ Are my paragraphs coherent and sentences manageable?

_____ ✔ Does my writing favor active voice and past tense?

_____ ✔ Does my conclusion mirror my opening argument?

_____ ✔ Have I taken care to use words appropriately?

_____ ✔ Is punctuation used according to common conventions?

_____ ✔ Are quotations clearly and appropriately set apart?

_____ ✔ When writing for a spoken presentation, have I altered the text appropriately?

------

[11]Linda K. Kerber, "Conference Rules: Everything You Need to Know about Presenting a Scholarly Paper in Public," *Perspectives on History: The Newsmagazine of the American Historical Association* 46, no. 5 (May 2008): 17–19.

DOCUMENTING SOURCES

■ ■ ■

After studying this chapter, you should be able to
- Identify four basic pieces of information for documenting any source.
- Compose appropriate note and bibliography citations.
- Prepare suitable short-form citations when necessary.
- Devise clear and complete citations to electronic sources.

When you write about history—or any other topic that requires research—you must use documentation that will allow readers to verify your sources. Indeed, to write history is always to write about sources. Your readers might want to check the evidence to see if you have cited it accurately and interpreted it soundly. Historians also use the documentation in books and articles they read to help them in their own research.

When you use information gathered from a source, tell your readers where to find the quotation or the information. When you quote the exact words of a source, enclose those words in quotation marks or use a block quotation to let readers know they are those of another author, and make a citation to the source of the quotation. If you summarize or paraphrase a source, let readers know what you are doing. Otherwise you may be guilty of plagiarism; always remember that plagiarism is the writer's unpardonable sin. Remember this: In a typical history essay of more than two or three pages, you will have many more citations to ideas and paraphrased information than you will to direct quotations.

A number of style manuals provide suggestions for forms of citations, including footnotes and endnotes. The conventional practice among historians, however, is to use the notes and bibliography formats suggested in

The Chicago Manual of Style, now in its sixteenth edition.[1] Generations of students have also used Kate L. Turabian, *A Manual for Writers of Term Papers, Theses, and Dissertations,*[2] a conveniently sized paperback condensation of the much more comprehensive *Chicago Manual of Style.* In addition to details concerning note citations and bibliographies, both guides provide suggestions about grammar, stylistic conventions, and information on parenthetical citations and associated reference lists that are frequently recommended to students in other disciplines. Because the format of note citations and bibliographies outlined in the *Chicago Manual* (and in Turabian's book) is the most widely used by historians, we have adopted that basic style for this brief guide to documenting your sources. We strongly endorse that historical convention because using notes—and especially footnotes—helps promote the historical conversation we mentioned in the first chapter. Unless you receive specific instructions to the contrary, we urge you to do the same.

At the end of this chapter we have included a "Writer's Checklist of Source Citations" providing samples of both note and bibliography formats of some common citation types most frequently used by historians. Turabian's manual is larger than this book, and as mentioned previously, it is only an abridgment of the much larger *Chicago Manual.* Both contain examples of citations for many more types of sources, and you should refer to them for additional advice. The good news is that common sense and care for precision and consistency can solve a multitude of problems and allow you to guide readers faithfully through the sources you have used, no matter what those sources may be.

BASIC PRINCIPLES

Whatever citation style you are expected to use, it must lead readers to the precise location of material quoted, summarized, or used as evidence in your essay. This requires that you pay particular attention to

---

[1] *The Chicago Manual of Style,* 16th ed. (Chicago: University of Chicago Press, 2010). A useful tool featuring examples of appropriate citations may be found at *The Chicago Manual of Style Online,* "Chicago-Style Citation Quick Guide," http://www.chicagomanualofstyle.org/tools_citationguide.html, then selecting the "Notes and Bibliography" tab; accessed 18 July 2013.

[2] Kate L. Turabian, *A Manual for Writers of Term Papers, Theses, and Dissertations,* 8th ed., rev. by Wayne C. Booth, Gregory G. Colomb, and Joseph M. Williams (Chicago: University of Chicago Press, 2013). This edition is keyed to the sixteenth edition of the *Chicago Manual.* A "Turabian Quick Guide" for citations is available at http://www.press.uchicago.edu/books/turabian/turabian_citationguide.html, then selecting the "Notes and Bibliography" tab; accessed 18 July 2013.

a number of details and make certain that they are presented carefully and consistently in your citations. Read Penny Sonnenburg's essay on Manifest Destiny in Appendix A. Notice the forms of citations she uses. Although some of her sources are mentioned in the text, for the most part she uses footnote citations in her essay. They could just as well have been placed at the end of the essay as endnotes. Some institutions and individual teachers, as well as book and journal publishers, prefer one over the other for a variety of reasons. From the writer's perspective, modern word processing programs make easy the formatting and placement of either footnotes or endnotes as well as the capacity to change from one to the other almost at will. We generally encourage the use of footnotes so that readers can quickly and easily discover your sources or, just as easily, pass over that information if they choose. If you are unsure which to use, ask your instructor. In our own experience, most instructors simply ask students to be consistent.

There are some basic principles you should always keep in mind when finding and taking notes from sources for your essay; you can also use these four basic categories to help you decide what information to include in citations of your documentation.

Authorship

The first principle to consider is authorship. Who created the work in question? Is there just one author, or are there several? Be sure to list multiple authors appropriately. Occasionally, a book may have an editor who is the principal creator of the work. Then, a bibliographic entry would look very similar to that for an authored book, while a note citation to one of the items within the book would be similar to that for any collection of essays. For a second entry by the same author or authors in a bibliography, replace the name with a dash (or underscore line) about six spaces long in place of the names; look at the "Select Bibliography of Student Resources" at the end of this book to see examples of how to do so.

A very few sources may have several individuals who contributed to the fundamental creation and presentation of the work. Most often these are editors and/or translators in addition to the main author; their names will be indicated prominently, usually on the title page of books and at the beginning (or occasionally at the end) of published articles. In recent years, some books—and especially texts—may have a long list of production credits on the same page as that including the publication data, as does this book. An editor mentioned there is not credited in a citation for that source. If there is no author named for a source, or if the source is acknowledged as being anonymous, begin your citation with the title.

Some authorship questions can be confusing. A book review, for example, has the reviewer as the principal author of that source, although the author of the book being reviewed should also be mentioned. In personal communications, such as letters or e-mails, the person writing should be listed first even though the person being written to is usually identified as well. Interviews are slightly more complex, as both the person being interviewed and the interviewer contribute directly to the creation of the interview. But since the person being interviewed is usually assumed to be the one supplying the crucial information (at least for historical research), the interviewee's name is listed first even though the name of the interviewer should be listed as well, if it is known.

Title(s)

The second basic element for each citation is the title. What is the source called? In the case of articles in a journal or newspaper, there will be more than a single title, one for the article and a second for the periodical. The complete title of a book or pamphlet should be in italics. Similarly, the title of a periodical—a scholarly journal, magazine, or newspaper—should be in italics. Italics are also used for motion pictures, paintings, sculptures, plays, blogs, and similar electronic works. But use quotation marks for short poems or speeches that have titles, just as you would for articles within a journal, magazine, or newspaper or in a collection of essays in book form. A few types of sources—such as interviews, letters, and manuscripts—are merely described in regular type without quotation marks. The same is true of Web site titles that are not otherwise titles of books, articles, or other works; however, an original essay within a Web site may be treated as an article and enclosed within quotation marks.

Location

Since a major purpose for the citation is that others may find the same work, the third important element in your citation should be the location where you found the information. For books, this means place of publication and the publisher. For scholarly journals, you will need to list the volume and sometimes the issue number (if the journal paginates each issue separately), and also the appropriate page numbers. For newspapers divided into sections, you usually include those section indicators in your citation as well as page numbers. Often Web sites and other electronic sources of information do not divide even long items into numbered sections or use page numbers. In such cases you need to use a discrete URL that will take a reader directly to the information you found. You may also want to indicate a search term or selection you used to find that information within the particular electronic file. (We have included further advice about citations for electronic sources later in this chapter.) For manuscripts, you will need to indicate both the collection name and the repository where they may be found, as well as any further location identifiers used by the repository or archive.

Date

The final element to consider is the date of your source. In the case of books, it is the year of publication; for journals, it is the year (and perhaps the month) of publication in addition to the volume and sometimes issue number. Newspaper and magazine citations usually have only the date and not volume and issue numbers. For Web sites, the date the particular source was created should be included; if the only date available is that of the most recent revision, that should be cited. Many reputable Web sites have such information clearly visible on the site; if no such dates are available, you should indicate *n.d.* for no date. Given concerns about the impermanence of URLs, many scholars suggest you also add the date you accessed the material on the Web; your instructors will appreciate knowing when in your research you located the item on the Web.

Shortened Forms for Subsequent Note Citations

When we first began our careers as historians, writers commonly used Latin abbreviations to make subsequent citations to sources they had already identified. This habit has gradually disappeared in academic writing, although both the *Chicago Manual* and Turabian's condensed guide still suggest it may be appropriate in limited cases to use *ibid* (for the Latin *ibidem,* "in the same place"). However, the increasing use of word processing programs which permit the easy movement of text—and the associated notes—from one location in an electronic file to another makes even that problematic. All too often we have found that notes transferred by the author from one location in an essay to another cannot easily be associated with their previous referents; hence, the meaning of a citation to *ibid* would not necessarily refer to the immediately preceding source. Thus, we recommend the exclusive use of shortened forms for subsequent citations. Should your instructor ask that you use *ibid* appropriately in your citations, do recheck your essay as it is finished to be certain that each time it appears it does refer to the immediately preceding source.

Such short forms can be both easily managed by authors and easily recognized by readers. In creating shortened references, you should use the author's (or authors') last name(s); you may, however, eliminate the names of translators and/or editors from subsequent references. If you use only one work from the same author(s) in your essay, then simply indicate the appropriate volume and page numbers in any subsequent note citation. But if you use more than one source by the same author you will also need to use a shortened title as well, of course keeping the original order of the words. However, for titles of three or four words, you can merely eliminate any initial article (*a, an,* or *the*) and use the entire title. In these cases, too, you should also include appropriate page references.

Use the sample citations in the "Writer's Checklist" at the end of this chapter as a guideline not just for the situations we have discussed, but also as models for other types of sources—keeping the basic principles for documenting sources in mind. And then compare your citations as well to the Turabian or *Chicago Manual* guides if you wish to be certain you have followed the usual historical conventions and have made them clear to your readers.

ELECTRONIC SOURCES

The availability of both primary and secondary source materials in electronic formats has caused historians to rethink some of their citations to such sources. In some cases these are merely digitized versions of printed (or in a few cases, handwritten) materials. In some cases, such as the electronic files of journal articles found in *JSTOR,* you should first make your citation to the original version and then indicate that you found the material on the Internet or in some other electronic form using the appropriate URL. Along with most historians, we would recommend that when you have a choice and can use either a printed or an electronic version of a source, you should opt for the printed version. But there are many source materials you will only be able to use in electronic formats, so it is essential that you learn to make full and complete citations to these in your essays.

The sixteenth edition of *The Chicago Manual of Style* makes numerous recommendations concerning citations of electronic sources, as does the eighth edition of Turabian. Most of the recommendations we make in this edition of our *Short Guide* follow those suggestions. Where our advice differs, we have tried to be clear by explaining our own recommendations. We have found that many other electronic citation guides are either based on other style manuals less familiar with historical conventions or on principles that address electronic technology issues more than concerns of historical writing. We urge you to follow our suggestions and those found in Turabian or the *Chicago Manual*; by all means check with your instructor as well.

We do recognize the Internet poses special problems for those who want to make fixed references to documents that are frequently less than permanent and subject to periodic alteration. In a key development to resolve some of these problems, digital object identifiers (DOIs)—similar in intent to ISBN numbers for books—are coming into greater use, but are not widely available or uniformly accepted as amendments to the more common uniform resource locators—URLs—with which you are familiar. Yet historians and humanists have for generations faced similar problems in citing sources. Private correspondence held by families of its recipients or in duplicate copies made by authors, for example, has long posed citation difficulties similar in nature to individual e-mail correspondence or, for that matter, materials in Web sites as well. And disappearing sources—such as long out of print books apparently not saved in any public repository or libraries and archives destroyed by fire—have also been of concern to writers who used such materials but whose readers may not be able to locate them. Using citations that include access dates, however, offers some assurance that you have looked carefully for electronic materials, even if they might later disappear from the Internet.

No method of citation can overcome these particular electronic citation problems, which, instead, cry out for great foresight in planning Web sites, careful explanations, and Web links to materials that may be moved, as well as acceptance of DOIs. Still, citation problems for electronic materials are, for the present, quite real. While historians should be concerned about such problems and make efforts to seek solutions, as a writer you cannot solve them. So move forward, keep the basic principles of any citation we have outlined in mind, and make your citations as clear and complete as you can.

There are certain conventions in the use of the Internet that writers of history should follow. While you may see angle (or pointed) brackets, < >, used to enclose either URLs or e-mail addresses, we urge you to put

URLs and e-mail addresses in normal type without any brackets or parentheses, keeping the punctuation as you find it. Nonetheless, some word processing programs may automatically convert these to hyperlinks on your screen. Often these hyperlinks are underlined and presented in a color font that may be reproduced if you merely print your file. If you are preparing printed versions of your essays, we suggest you remove the hyperlinks. To do so, move your cursor onto the link using the arrow keys on your keyboard and then use word processing EDIT functions to remove the hyperlink. Often you may click on your right mouse button to do this.

Standard Internet practice is also to put the URL on a single, separate line, if possible. But in printed citations it is often preferable for the address to continue from one line to another. When doing so, we recommend following the advice offered by Turabian and the *Chicago Manual* that you end a line of text with any double slash (//) or colon (:), but that you carry a single slash (/), period, comma, underline (_), or tilde (~) on to the next line of text. You may elect to place an equals sign (=) or ampersand (&) on either line, but should avoid making any break at a hyphen (-) if there is one in the URL. You should include any final slash in the URL, but don't carry it to another line; readers will usually understand that any other punctuation following the URL belongs to your sentence. You may include e-mail addresses in your text by breaking them at the end of a line in similar fashion, if necessary.

Even these suggestions will not solve the problem of complex URLs, which are generated when you use some search utilities. Often the resulting electronic addresses are at best unmanageable in citations; frequently they may not even be useful as hyperlinks allowing readers to reach the same site. The stable URLs generated by some high-quality databases, such as JSTOR, are appropriate for citations. Other search utilities, such as those designed to find information *within* large and extensive Web sites, present different problems. For example, using the search utility on the main H-Net Web site to locate information concerning the online archive of the Central London Criminal Court, known as the Old Bailey, could result in finding messages in the H-Net discussion logs containing that digitized resource. One of these messages, posted by Dave Featherstone to the H-Atlantic discussion forum in March 2003, is identified by this URL: http://h-net. msu.edu/cgi-bin/logbrowse.pl?trx=vx&list=h-atlantic &month =0303 &week=c&msg=kNjii8wX74ykTVNHLzS/AQ&user=&pw=. In this case, the URL generated by the search might be used independently to retrieve the document, but it is clearly unwieldy at best when put into print. On this conundrum neither Turabian's eighth edition nor the *Chicago Manual's* sixteenth edition offers clear guidance.

There is, however, a very simple solution, which is comparable to a similar circumstance in using print sources. This involves use of the abbreviation *s.v.* (for the Latin *sub verbo,* "under the word") in making citations to standard reference works such as encyclopedias and dictionaries, which are organized into individual entries usually presented in alphabetical order. Doing so in the electronic citation just mentioned would refer to the main URL of the Web site that included the search function, then would indicate to the reader that the particular message could be found by entering the words "Old Bailey online" in that internal search utility:

> Dave Featherstone, "Proceedings of Old Bailey
> Online," message to H-Atlantic, 15 March 2003,
> in H-Net: Humanities and Social Sciences Online,
> http://www.h-net.org, s.v. "Old Bailey online,"
> accessed 20 July 2013.

Both the *Chicago Manual* and Turabian suggest that such citations employing *s.v.* should only be used in notes and not in bibliographies. We believe that in the case of electronic sources—although NOT for printed encyclopedias and dictionaries—using such a citation format even in bibliographies, if necessary, offers writers an appropriate solution to one of the difficulties posed in documenting modern electronic sources.

One word of caution: We do NOT recommend that you make such citations to materials you find using one of the Internet-wide search engines such as *Google, bing,* or *Yahoo!* Those search utilities take you to individual Web sites, which you should document separately. To make your citation to the search engine itself would be as if you made a citation to a book by merely referring to the library catalog in which you had first found a reference to it! Only use the *s.v.* (or *s.vv.* for multiple search terms) format for electronic searches you make from the home page of a particular Web site that contains within it the material you have used in your essay, whether using that Web site's search utility or an EDIT command on your Web browser to "find (on this page)."

Citations to e-mail and listerv messages also present problems, although even these have analogs in well-accepted conventions for the citation of similar sources. The person writing is clearly the author, although the person or group receiving the message should be noted as well, along with the date of the communication. Many listserv messages are available in some form of publicly available electronic archive, such as the H-Net archive we previously mentioned. If so, you should document the archived version in your citation; if there is no archive, the citation would end with the date. Precisely because so many listserv and e-mail messages are not available to most researchers in an electronic archive, some historians eschew them as sources. Yet just as historians may occasionally wish to document information received in private letters they have received, you may need to document such unarchived messages to an electronic mailing list or even in a private e-mail message that may have served as a valuable source for your essay. Some historians do insist on including the author's e-mail address as a means of verifying the information, although you should never do so without permission.

Despite the difficulties, we are confident that solutions to documentation problems for source material on the Internet and in other electronic formats are possible. Don't simply avoid such sources for lack of standard conventions for making citations to them. Ask your instructor's advice about how you might best make citations to electronic sources, and use the citation samples in the "Writer's Checklist" at the end of this chapter as guides to documenting your use of all the sources you have consulted in writing your essay.

NOTES AND BIBLIOGRAPHIES

In historical writing, the conventional forms for citing sources have long been notes and bibliographies. While both present essentially the same information in similar ways, they do serve different functions. Notes are written in the same manner, whether they are presented as footnotes—at the bottom of each page where the citation occurs—or as endnotes—at the end of the essay, before the bibliography. Of course, each note should be preceded by a number referring to the place in your essay where you want to document sources for what you have written. These numbers, both in the text and at the start of each note, are best set as superscript numerals, something easily achieved with a word processing program. Each note should begin with a paragraph indent so it can easily be distinguished in your text. A style for presenting citation information in notes has evolved over the years, and that presented in the "Writers Checklist" at the end of this chapter, in the *Chicago Manual,* and in *Turabian* has become the conventional standard for historians.

This style and format for notes allows quick, easy reading, especially at the bottom of a page of text, but also in quick glances at a list positioned at the end of the essay or book. Readers want to know why an author's story is intended to be true. Convince them by making clear what evidence you used to support your statements and connecting that information directly to what you write. Historians use notes to do this, and you should as well. Notes also help readers search for the same specific bits of information they read about, should they wish to do so. You should take similar advantage of the notes you find in your sources when preparing to write your own essays. Making a practice of doing so will not only aid your research but will also help in learning how to prepare notes for your own essays.

Bibliographies, on the other hand, are more formal. While these citations use much the same information as notes, they are alphabetized by the last name of the author, and the punctuation is somewhat different. For a second work by the same author(s), use a six-space line to replace the name(s); the "Select Bibliography of Student Resources" at the end of this book provides examples of how to do this. If there is no author, bibliographic citations begin with the title, which is used for alphabetizing such entries along with others. You will also find examples of bibliographic citations in the "Writer's Checklist" at the end of this chapter.

Bibliographies are placed at the end of an essay or book to allow readers to see quickly what works have been cited or consulted by the author. A bibliography shows whether the writer has searched a wide variety of sources and whether he or she knows the latest literature in a field of inquiry. But some individual items are not generally included in a bibliography even though you may have cited them in note citations; there are samples of several such citations in the "Writer's Checklist." If you have questions, be sure to consult with your instructor about what you should include in your bibliography; sometimes only sources cited in your essay should be included, but often a full list of the materials consulted is more appropriate. You may sometimes be asked to make your research efforts clearer by presenting an annotated bibliography, which includes a brief comment on the contents of the book, article, or other source. If you do annotate your bibliography, follow the model in the "Select Bibliography of Student Resources" at the end of this book.

Writer's Checklist of Source Citations

Use these citation samples in your own historical writing by matching the types of sources you have used to the following categories, selecting either Bibliography or Note formats; the latter also includes samples of subsequent note references. These samples represent citations for some of the most common types of sources you are likely to encounter. Our suggestions follow those offered by Kate Turabian, her successors, and the editors of *The Chicago Manual of Style*; we have discussed our recommendations previously in this chapter, including slight modifications in a very few cases.

book (single author)

B   Maxson, Brian J. *The Humanist World of Renaissance Florence.* Cambridge: Cambridge University Press, 2014.

N   [1] Brian J. Maxson, *The Humanist World of Renaissance Florence* (Cambridge: Cambridge University Press, 2014), 156.

[2] Maxson, 121.

book (author named in title)

B   *The Autobiography of Benjamin Franklin.* Edited by John Bigelow. 3 vols. 1874. Reprint, Cambridge and New York: Cambridge University Press, 2011.

N   [1] *The Autobiography of Benjamin Franklin*, edited by John Bigelow, 3 vols. (1874; repr. Cambridge and New York: Cambridge University Press, 2011), 2:275.

[2] *Autobiography of Benjamin Franklin*, 1:37.

book (two authors)

B   Engerman, Stanley L. and Robert W. Fogel. *Time on the Cross: The Economics of American Negro Slavery.* New York: Norton, 1989.

N   [1] Stanley L. Engerman and Robert W. Fogel, *Time on the Cross: The Economics of American Negro Slavery* (New York: Norton, 1989), 206.

[2] Engerman and Fogel, 208.

book (multiple authors)

B   Muzuli, Bakili, Yusuf M. Juwayeyi, Mercy Makhambera, and Desmond D. Phiri. *Democracy with a Price: The History of Malawi since 1900.* Blantyre, Malawi: Jhango Heinemann, 1999.

N   [1] Bakili Muluzi, *et al.*, *Democracy with a Price: The History of Malawi since 1900* (Blantyre, Malawi: Jhango Heinemann, 1999), 17.

         [2] Muluzi, 19.

book (subsequent edition)

B   Thornton, John. *Africa and Africans in the Making of the Atlantic World, 1400–1800*, 2d ed. Cambridge and New York: Cambridge University Press, 1998.

N   [1] John Thornton, *Africa and Africans in the Making of the Atlantic World, 1400–1800*, 2d ed. (Cambridge and New York: Cambridge University Press, 1998), 157.

         [2] Thornton, *Africa and Africans*, 159.

book (reprint edition)

B   Washington, Booker T. *The Future of the American Negro.* n.p.: Small, Maynard & Co., 1899. Reprint, New York: New American Library, 1969.

N   [1] Booker T. Washington, *The Future of the American Negro* (n.p.: Small, Maynard & Co., 1899; repr. New York: New American Library, 1969), 17. Citations are to the reprint edition.

         [2] Washington, 26.

book (editor as author)

B   Hilliard, Constance B., ed. *Intellectual Traditions of Pre-Colonial Africa.* Boston: McGraw-Hill, 1998.

N   [1] Constance B. Hilliard, ed., *Intellectual Traditions of Pre-Colonial Africa* (Boston: McGraw-Hill, 1998), 4.

         [2] Hilliard, 10.

book (author/editor unnamed)

B   *Cultures and Time.* Paris: The Unesco Press, 1976.

N   [1] *Cultures and Time* (Paris: The Unesco Press, 1976), 7.

         [2] *Cultures and Time*, 9.

book (edited or translated)

B   Luther, Martin. *Lectures on Romans.* Edited and translated by Wilhelm Pauck. Philadelphia: Westminster Press, 1961.

N   [1] Martin Luther, *Lectures on Romans*, ed. and trans. Wilhelm Pauck (Philadelphia: Westminster Press, 1961), 101.

         [2] Luther, 76.

book in a series

B   Post, Robert C. *Technology, Transport, and Travel in American History.* Historical Perspectives on Technology, Society, and Culture. Washington, DC: American Historical Association, 2003.

N   [1] Robert C. Post, *Technology, Transport, and Travel in American History,* Historical Perspectives on Technology, Society, and Culture (Washington, DC: American Historical Association, 2003), 53.

    [2] Post, 54.

pamphlet

B   South Africa. Department of Education. *The South African History Project.* Pretoria: Department of Education, ca. 2001.

N   [1] South Africa, Department of Education, *The South African History Project* (Pretoria: Department of Education, ca. 2001), 2.

    [2] *South African History Project,* 3.

article in a book of essays

B   Spiegel, Gabrielle. "History and postmodernism." In *The Postmodern History Reader,* ed. Keith Jenkins, 260–73. London and New York: Routledge, 1997.

N   [1] Gabrielle Spiegel, "History and postmodernism," in *The Postmodern History Reader,* ed. Keith Jenkins (London and New York: Routledge, 1997), 261.

    [2] Spiegel, 263.

article in a scholarly journal

B   Spooner, Denise S. "A New Perspective on the Dream: Midwestern Images of Southern California in the Post–World War II Decades." *California History* 76, no. 1 (Spring 1997): 45–57.

N   [1] Denise S. Spooner, "A New Perspective on the Dream: Midwestern Images of Southern California in the Post–World War II Decades," *California History* 76, no. 1 (Spring 1997): 45.

    [2] Spooner, 48

article in a popular magazine

B   McGlynn, Sean. "Violence and the Law in Medieval England." *History Today,* April 2008, 53–59.

N   [1] Sean McGlynn, "Violence and the Law in Medieval England," *History Today,* April 2008, 57.

    [2] McGlynn, 54.

article in popular magazine (author/editor unnamed)

B   "War Letters," *National Geographic,* November 2005, 78–95.

N   [1] "War Letters," *National Geographic,* November 2005, 92.

   [2] "Letters," 89.

article in an online magazine

B   Conniff, Richard. "What the Luddites Really Fought Against."
   Smithsonian, March 2011. http://www.smithsonianmag.com/history-
   archaeology/What-the-Luddites-Really-Fought-Against.html,
   accessed 10 March 2011.

N   [1] Richard Conniff, "What the Luddites Really Fought Against."
   Smithsonian, March 2011, http://www.smithsonianmag.com/history-
   archaeology/What-the-Luddites-Really-Fought-Against.html,
   accessed 10 March 2011.

   [2] Conniff.

article in a newspaper

B   Sanger, David E. "Clinton Warns Japan: Fire Up Economy to Stem a
   Decline." *New York Times,* 4 April 1998, A1.

N   [1] David E. Sanger, "Clinton Warns Japan: Fire Up Economy to Stem
   a Decline," *New York Times,* 4 April 1998, A1.

   [2] Sanger.

article in a newspaper (author unnamed)

B   "Science Jottings: Trench Fever." *The Illustrated London News,*
   28 October 1916, 516.

N   [1] "Science Jottings: Trench Fever," *The Illustrated London News,*
   28 October 1916, 516.

   [2] "Trench Fever."

reference work

B   Wiener, Philip P., ed. *Dictionary of the History of Ideas.* Five volumes.
   New York: Scribner's, 1973.

entry in a reference work

N   [1] *Dictionary of the History of Ideas, s.v.* "Historiography," by Herbert
   Butterfield, 465.

   [2] Butterfield, 465.

entry in a reference work (author unnamed)

N [1] *Encyclopedia of World History*, s.vv. "computer, history of the," 157.
[2] "History of the Computer," 158.

thesis or dissertation (unpublished)

B Vasconcellos, Colleen A. "'And a child shall lead them?': slavery, childhood, and African cultural identity in Jamaica, 1750–1838." PhD dissertation, Florida International University, 2004.

N [1] Colleen A. Vasconcellos, "'And a child shall lead them?': slavery, childhood, and African cultural identity in Jamaica, 1750–1838" (PhD dissertation, Florida International University, 2004), 72.
[2] Vasconcellos, 27.

thesis or dissertation (available online)

B Horton, Justin G. "The Second Lost Cause: Post-National Confederate Imperialism in the Americas." MA thesis, East Tennessee State University, 2007. http://libraries.etsu.edu/ record=b2113028, accessed 4 June 2008.

N [1] Justin G. Horton, "The Second Lost Cause: Post-National Confederate Imperialism in the Americas" (MA thesis, East Tennessee State University, 2007), 43, http://libraries.etsu.edu/record=b2113028, accessed 4 June 2008.
[2] Horton, 16.

archive collection

B Bowman Family Collection. Accession No. 23, Archives of Appalachia, East Tennessee State University. Johnson City, TN.

archive document

N [1] Benjamin Bowman, manuscript letter to Joseph Bowman, 24 July 1860, Bowman Family Collection, acc. No. 23, Archives of Appalachia, East Tennessee State University, Johnson City, TN.
[2] B. Bowman to J. Bowman, 24 Jul 1860.

book review

B Ze'evi, Dror. Review of *Desiring Arabs*, by Joseph A. Massad. *The American Historical Review* 113 (2008): 1480–81.

N   [1] Dror Ze'evi, review of *Desiring Arabs*, by Joseph A. Massad,
         The American Historical Review 113 (2008): 1480.

         [2] Ze'evi, review of Massad, 1481.

government document (online)

B   U.S. National Archives and Records Administration. "Pictures of
         World War II." College Park, MD, National Archives and Records
         Administration, 2004. http://www.archives.gov/research /military/
         ww2/photos/, accessed 10 March 2011.

N   [1] U.S. National Archives and Records Administration, "Pictures
         of World War II" (College Park, MD, National Archives and Records
         Administration, 2004), http://www.archives.gov/research/military/ww2/
         photos/, accessed 10 March 2011.

         [2] NARA, "Pictures of World War II."

Web site document (separate URL)

B   Miller, Joseph C. "History and Africa/Africa and History." 8 January
         1999. http://www.ecu.edu/African/sersas/jmahapa.htm, accessed 23
         November 2003.

N   [1] Joseph C. Miller, "History and Africa/Africa and History"
         (8 January 1999) http://www.ecu.edu/African/sersas/jmahapa.htm,
         accessed 4 June 2008.

         [2] Miller.

Web site document (accessed through internal search)

B   Hoover, Irwin H. Memoir. 4 March 1913. In Library of Congress:
         American Memory, http://memory.loc.gov, *s.v.* "Irwin H. Hoover,"
         accessed 27 April 2005.

N   [1] Irwin H. Hoover, memoir, 4 March 1913, in Library of Congress:
         American Memory, http://memory.loc.gov/index.html *s.v.* "Irwin H.
         Hoover," accessed 27 April 2005.

         [2] Hoover.

unpublished paper

B   Rosenfeld, Gavriel D. "Alternate History and Memory." Paper presented
         at annual meeting of American Historical Association, Philadelphia,
         6 January 2006.

N   [1] Gavriel D. Rosenfeld, "Alternate History and Memory" (paper
         presented at annual meeting of American Historical Association,
         Philadelphia, 6 January 2006).

         [2] Rosenfeld.

motion picture (video/DVD)

B   *Breaker Morant.* Videocassette. Directed by Bruce Beresford. 1979. Burbank, CA: RCA/Columbia Pictures Home Video, 1985.

N   [1] *Breaker Morant*, videocassette, directed by Bruce Beresford (1979; Burbank, CA: RCA/Columbia Pictures Home Video, 1985).

[2] *Breaker Morant*, 1985.

television or radio program (online archived)

B   "NASCAR Challenge." *American Pickers.* Aired on 11 April 2011, on The History Channel. http://www.history.com/shows/american-pickers/videos/american-pickers-nascar-challenge, accessed 31 July 2011.

N   [1] "NASCAR Challenge," *American Pickers*, originally aired 11 April 2011, on The History Channel, http://www.history.com/shows/american-pickers/videos/american-pickers-nascar-challenge, accessed 31 July 2013.

[2] "NASCAR Challenge."

television or radio broadcast (on air)

B   Wertheimer, Linda. "Ex. Rep. Lindy Boggs: Advocate For Women, Dedicated To Family." *Weekend Edition Saturday.* Aired 25 July 2013 on National Public Radio.

N   [1] Linda Wertheimer, "Ex. Rep. Lindy Boggs: Advocate For Women, Dedicated To Family," *Weekend Edition Saturday*, National Public Radio, aired 25 July 2013.

[2] Wertheimer, "Lindy Boggs."

interview

N   [1] Stambuli Likuleka, interview by Melvin E. Page, 17 August 1972.

[2] Likuleka interview.

photograph

N   [1] Ken Geiger, "Stonehenge, weathered and broken," photograph, *National Geographic*, June 2008, 59.

[2] Geiger, "Stonehenge" (photograph).

photograph (photographer unnamed)

N   [1] "An excellent example of a pack or artillery mule," photograph, in *Shavetails & Bell Sharpes: The History of the U. S. Army Mule*, by Emmett M. Essin (Lincoln: University of Nebraska Press, 1997), facing p. 85.

[2] Photograph in Essin, 85.

work of art

N   [1] Jan van Eyck, *Giovanni Arnolfini and His Bride*, painting, as reproduced in Dennis Sherman et al., *World Civilizations: Sources, Images, and Interpretations*, 3rd ed. (New York: McGraw-Hill, 2002), 1: 231.

[2] van Eyck, *Giovanni Arnolfini and His Bride*.

message in Internet discussion list/blog

N   [1] Richard Lobban, "REPLY: African Muslim Slaves in America," message to H-Africa, h-africa@msu.edu, 4 August 1995, archived at http://www.h-net.org /~africa/archives/august95.

[2] Lobban.

private letter

N   [1] George Shepperson, letter to author, 4 October 2004.

private e-mail message

N   [1] Carol Jones, e-mail message to author, 16 July 2009.

one source quoted in another

N   [1] Frank Dupuis, "A Nobody in a Forgotten Campaign," typescript (ca. 1972), privately held, quoted in Melvin E. Page, *The Chiwaya War: Malawians and the First World War* (Boulder, CO: Westview Press, 2000), 109.

[2] Dupuis.

APPENDIX A

■ ■ ■

Sample Student Research Paper

On the following pages you will find a sample research paper written for a course in world history using the process we have outlined in this book (and sometimes illustrating it with Ms. Sonnenburg's experiences). Study the paper. Then consider the questions about the paper at the end. Ask similar questions about any essay you write for a history course.

Pay close attention to the format of the paper. Note the title page, the footnotes, and the bibliography. The title page includes the title of the paper, the name of the author, the date the paper is turned in, the name of the course, the time of the class, and the name of the professor. The margins should be set at no less than one inch on all four sides of the page. *Always* number pages, but remember that the title page is not numbered, although it is considered page one in the text of your paper.

Manifest Destiny: A Characteristic of Nations

BY PENNY M. SONNENBURG
East Tennessee State University
March 20, 2003
History 4957: Colonialism and Imperialism
Professor Melvin Page
M 2:00—4:50 pm

More than a century before John L. O'Sullivan wrote the words reflective of the expansionist fervor that gripped the United States, of "our manifest destiny to overspread the continent,"[1] the essence of the idea was already a part of what would become our national heritage. Yet as late as the 1920s, Julius Pratt proclaimed confidently in *The American Historical Review* that O'Sullivan invented the phrase.[2] Now, over a century and a half after O'Sullivan penned those well-known words, it should be apparent that the United States was not alone in its fervor and O'Sullivan merely gave dramatic voice to what was a well-developed national disposition with deep roots in the western tradition.

In *The Power of Ideals in American History*, Ephraim Adams construed the concept of "manifest destiny" as inherent in the nature of nearly all countries, dispelling the notion that it was a unique American characteristic. Adams elaborated that the "sense of destiny is an attribute of all nations and all peoples." He claimed that if we penetrated beyond recorded history, distinct emotions of various tribes and races would provide an early understanding of "manifest destiny." Probably we would find that these tribes and races also felt themselves a "chosen people" set apart for some high purpose.[3]

Adams also implied that any great nation had a belief in its destiny; larger nations wanted a place in the sun while smaller, contented nations were constantly on alert to avoid absorption by

---

[1] John L. O'Sullivan, "Annexation," *Democratic Review* 17 (July and August 1845), quoted in *Manifest Destiny and the Imperialism Question*, ed. Charles L. Sanford (New York: John Wiley & Sons, 1974), 28.

[2] Julius W. Pratt, "The Origin of 'Manifest Destiny,'" *The American Historical Review* 32 (1927): 798.

[3] Ephraim Douglas Adams, *The Power of Ideals in American History* (New York: AMS Press, Inc. 1969), 67.

their more powerful neighbors. As historians, we can analyze and thereby illustrate that the concept of manifest destiny occurred long before 1845 and was not limited to the American people. The United States, beginning with its colonial past, utilized the essence of the concept placing it on a higher philosophical plane. The nationalistic expansionist movement in the United States was based upon a moral ideology and appeared as an inherent quality justifying itself as a natural right.[4]

Natural right formed the historical foundation that was later used as an explanation and underlying ideology surrounding the manifest destiny movement. Natural right was basically defined as any right that "nature," recognized in a "divinely supported system of 'natural law' inclusive of moral truths, bestows prior to or independently of political society." The beginnings of this idea can be traced back to Greek philosophers who wrote of "things that are right by nature, that is, inherently, and can be recognized by every rational being to be so."[5] Later stoic philosophers, and indeed basic Roman legal beliefs, followed the same reasoning that natural rights were among the truths contained in natural law. Sir Ernest Barker, in *Traditions of Civility,* addressed the natural law idea as a movement among the Stoic thinkers of the Hellenistic age. The large and somewhat general expression "became a tradition of human civility which runs continuously from the Stoic teachers of the Porch to the American Revolution of 1776 and the French Revolution of 1789."[6] For many centuries this was directly considered part and parcel of church theology, later adopted by the Catholic Church and forming a core element of

---

[4]Albert K. Weinberg, *Manifest Destiny: A Study of Nationalist Expansionism in American History* (New York: Johns Hopkins Press, 1958), 12.

[5]Weinberg, 13-14.

[6]Ernest Barker, *Traditions of Civility* (Cambridge: Cambridge University Press, 1948), 312.

APPENDIX A ■ *Sample Student Research Paper* **147**

church doctrine for teachers and early canonists.
This logic formed a rational basis for the physical
and moral universe, hence the "theory of Natural
Law had become in the sixteenth century, and
continued to remain during the seventeenth and
the eighteenth, an independent and rationalist
system professed and expounded by the philosophers
of the secular school of natural law."[7] Later,
Christianity "harmonized these ideas of paganism
with its own theology by regarding natural law as
the expression of the eternal reason of God." And
thus natural right came to embrace two principles
in the western tradition—secular and sacred—and set
the stage for the "momentous pretension later to
be called nationalism." This powerful affirmation
enhanced an emerging idea that nationalities were
the most likely agencies for promoting not only
the rights of particular groups, but also the
rights of mankind as a whole.[8] This tendency toward
an assertion of group entitlement confirmed for
Adams his view of early tribes and races employing
concepts of higher purpose, foreshadowing early
nationalistic leanings.

Based on this *a priori* condition, there is
firm ground for asserting the close relationships between the ideas usually described as
nationalism, expansionism, ethnicity, natural
law, and manifest destiny. The rhetoric of politics, religion, and philosophy throughout early
European history established a touchstone for these
relationships. And early historians of Europe were
instrumental in drawing attention to the connections. Tacitus, a Roman historian of the Germanic
peoples, described in his *Germania* such characteristics among the people about whom he wrote. "The
tribes of Germany," he declared, "are free from
all taint of intermarriages with foreign nations,
and . . . they appear as a distinct, unmixed race,

---

[7]Barker, 216.
[8]Weinberg, 13-14.

like none but themselves."[9] Such tendencies were
passed on to the early populations of Great Britain
who were descendants of Germanic tribes. William
Camden confirms this in his *Remaines concerning
Britaine*, writing that "he saw God's hand in the
guiding of the Angles and Saxons to England."[10]
This version of the "chosen people" doctrine became
an early cornerstone of popular ideology in England
as the New Anglican church under Elizabeth adopted
the essence of its message.

Archbishop Matthew Parker, a major defender of
Anglo-Saxon literature and scholarship, along with
his secretary, John Joscelyn, began an inquiry of
pre-Norman English history. The purpose of their
study was an effort not only to prove the ancient-
ness of new English church customs but also to
promote an interest in general English history
during the Anglo-Saxon period. Archbishop Parker's
contemporary, John Foxe, particularly emphasized
in his 1563 *Acts and Monuments* the "uniqueness of
the English and their nature as 'a chosen people,'
with a church lineage stretching back to Joseph of
Arimathea and his supposed visit to England, and
with John Wyclif as the true originator of the Ref-
ormation."[11] Following the English Revolution, and
especially after the Restoration of the monarchy,
"the idea of the English nation as the crusading
agent of God's will faded" into a minor theme in
English thought. But the historical roots of the
philosophy ran deep and were planted especially
on the frontiers of English expansionism. It is no
wonder then, that "Americans never lost the belief

---

[9]Tacitus, *The Agricola and Germania*, trans.
A. J. Church and W. J. Brodribb (London: Macmillan,
1877), in Medieval Source Book, ed. Paul Halsall,
http://www.fordham.edu/halsall/source/tacitus1.
html, January 1996, accessed 17 February 2003.

[10]Quoted in Reginald Horsman, *Race and Manifest
Destiny* (Cambridge: Harvard University Press,
1981), 12.

[11]Horsman, 10.

that they were a special, chosen people, a people destined to change the world for the better."[12]

The ascendancy of the English view of the Anglo-Saxons appeared as an inherent characteristic in the American colonies. The post-Reformation Continental writers reinforced the myth produced by two centuries of political and religious conflict. "As colonial Englishmen the settlers in America fully absorbed the mythical view of the English past developed between 1530 and 1730."[13] Colonial settlers did not limit their absorption to one viewpoint. They also embraced and were inspired by an emerging philosophy of nationalism. In an effort to systematize nationalism, eighteenth-century European philosophers provided the spark for revolutionary movements of the period. The diversity of thought found in the "culturally nationalistic Herder, the democratic Rousseau, the Tory Bolingbroke, and the liberal physiocrats" was transplanted into the natural rights domain of the American colonial psyche. These philosophers' proto-nationalist doctrines basically included one—and usually both—of two basic foundations of natural right ideas. The first principle addressed the "natural rights of groups to determine upon and organize the desired form of government." The second principle declared that nations were the "natural agencies" for advancing not only the rights of particular groups but also the rights of all mankind.[14] One does not have to have an overactive imagination to recognize this characteristic in colonial America.

In *Manifest Destiny and Mission in American History, a Reinterpretation,* historian Frederick Merk links nationalism with expansionism. He asserts that expansionism was usually associated with ideology. Merk's validation of this point leads one past the early writings of natural right

---

[12]Horsman, 82.
[13]Horsman, 15.
[14]Weinberg, 13-14.

into an ideological framework for expansionism. His broad, global sweeps through expansionist ideology are summarized as he concludes of the causes: "in the case of Arab expansionism it was Islam; in Spanish expansionism, Catholicism; in Napoleonic expansionism, revolutionary liberalism; in Russian and Chinese expansionism, Marxian communism." In the United States an equivalent of these ideologies appeared as manifest destiny, and the main ingredients consisted of republicanism, democracy, freedom of religion, and Anglo-Saxonism.[15] The intellectual ship that carried the settlers across the wide Atlantic also altered and then adopted the "idea of natural right as the moral rationale of America's expansionism." In the early developmental period, the newly arrived Americans tended to stress the rights rather than the duties of natural law. "The conception of natural right was first used by New England clergymen in behalf of right of ecclesiastical independency." In 1760 the concept escaped from the pulpits into the public discussion arena as Americans became concerned with their own political rights under English rule. This ideological transformation reached an initial climax with inclusion of the "inalienable natural rights with which their Creator had endowed them [Americans]" in the Declaration of Independence confirming the United States' belief in its "chosenness." Americans assumed the position "among the powers of the earth, the separate and equal station to which the Laws of Nature and Nature's God entitle them." Assuming the position of natural rights guardian, Americans justified the "right of revolution when governments became destructive of natural rights."[16]

The end of the American Revolution empowered the new nation and set it along a course

---

[15]Frederick Merk, *Manifest Destiny and Mission in American History, A Reinterpretation* (New York: Alfred A. Knopf, 1963), vii–ix.
[16]Weinberg, 16.

that engaged the country in the manifest destiny phenomenon. This total embrace of a powerful movement allowed the misnomer that manifest destiny was a unique American feature. Early American history is laced with examples of the doctrine that have been used throughout as situational justification of the means to the end. In 1801 Jefferson's application of diplomatic and military pressure induced Napoleon to negotiate with the United States for the sale of New Orleans and a slice of coastal territory to the east. Much to Jefferson's surprise, in 1803 Napoleon sold all of the immense Louisiana territory to the United States. This enabled Jefferson to realize his main objective: possession of New Orleans and ultimate control of the mouth of the Mississippi, thus providing the much-needed outlet to world markets for the interior of the new nation.[17] Acquisition of the Louisiana Purchase also perpetuated the expansionist movement of the United States.

This expansionism continued as a nationally heartfelt but nameless movement. As early as 1818 Andrew Jackson applied his own understanding of President Monroe's instructions and led military forces into Spanish-held Florida destroying the Indians in his path; he set into motion the natural rights claim of Americans to possession of any land that they wanted.[18] Further use of the still unnamed principle appeared as an American assumption that its destiny was that of a world power. In 1822 the Monroe Doctrine—warning the whole of Europe to stay out of the Western Hemisphere—illustrated James Monroe's belief in this idea. Monroe was certainly not alone in this belief, although there was a small vocal opposition, which made the still unnamed doctrine a disputed philosophy.

---

[17]David Goldfield et al., *The American Journey, A History of the United States* (Upper Saddle River, NJ: Prentice Hall, 1998), 261.
[18]Goldfield et al., 277.

The opposition movement exposed a different side to Americans as being the "chosen people." In an 1837 letter to Henry Clay, William E. Channing—the social activist and leading figure in the American Unitarian movement—wrote that "we are a restless people, prone to encroachment, impatient of the ordinary laws of progress." Channing feared the strength that the country felt at extending its boundaries—by natural right—from shore to shore was fraught with dire consequences. "We boast of our rapid growth," he continued in his letter to Clay, "forgetting that, throughout nature, noble growths are slow.... Already endangered by our greatness, we cannot advance without imminent peril to our institutions, union, prosperity, virtue, and peace.... There is no fate to justify rapacious nations, any more than to justify gamblers and robbers, in plunder."[19] Opposition, however, seems to have emboldened the proponents of the doctrine which was only then surfacing in open expression.

What seemed to be the opinion of a majority of the American people at the time was featured not only in John O'Sullivan's 1845 editorial in the *Democratic Review,* but also in another article published in the same journal that year. This also addressed the Texas annexation issue and justified the addition of the new state. "Texas has been absorbed into the Union in the inevitable fulfillment of the general law which is rolling our population westward." O'Sullivan contended that Texas "was disintegrated from Mexico in the natural course of events, by a process perfectly legitimate on its Union was not only inevitable, but the most natural, right and proper thing in the world."[20] It is not ironic that the article appeared in this

---

[19]Quoted in Michael T. Lubragge, "Manifest Destiny: The Philosophy That Created a Nation," in From Revolution to Reconstruction, http://odur.let.rug.nl/~usa/E/manifest/manif1.htm, updated 6 March 2003, accessed 12 March 2003.

[20]Quoted in Lubragge, "Manifest Destiny."

particular *Review,* as it was the same journal that finally gave a name—hence a formal justification— for what was believed the right of Americans: our Manifest Destiny.

Precursors to American predominance had been played out, and history was set to be made, all in the name of Manifest Destiny. This is a classic example of how, when doctrines gain names, they in turn gain legitimacy and ultimately power. The combination of the idealistic vision of social perfection through God and the pride of American nationalism in the mid-nineteenth century filled an American ideological need for domination of the hemisphere from pole to pole, as Monroe had implied. This was ultimately based on the concept of Americans possessing a divine providence. The strong belief of God's will for American expansion over the whole of the continent and to ultimately control the country led to a guiding call to human destiny. "It was white man's burden to conquer and christianize the land," as Kipling envisioned at the end of the nineteenth century. This expanded the Puritan notion of a "city on a hill" and was secularized into Manifest Destiny, albeit a materialistic, religious, and utopian destiny.[21]

This eventually led to the fear that foreigners crossing the national frontier borders might hamper the security of the United States. The most reasonable answer was to conquer land beyond those borders and expand to other areas. This became evident when Albert T. Beveridge arose in the U.S. Senate and espoused the view—with utmost certainty— that "Anglo-Saxon [America] was destined to rule the world" and went on to state that "He [God] has made us the master organizers of the world to establish system where chaos reigns."[22] In speaking so boldly, Beveridge introduced an international dimension to American Manifest Destiny that

---

[21]Lubragge, "Manifest Destiny."
[22]Quoted in Lubragge, "Manifest Destiny."

justified the 1867 purchase of Alaska from Russia for $7,200,000. The price of being a world empire had risen since the earlier purchase of Louisiana from Napoleon! Indeed, not only the price but the arrogance of this doctrine was on the rise as the expansionist fervor grew following the Spanish-American War. Congress went so far as to call for annexation of all Spanish territories. Newspapers of the time were more extreme in suggesting the annexation of Spain itself.

Aspirations of an American empire were echoed in the views of other expansionists including Theodore Roosevelt, former President Harrison, and Captain Alfred T. Mahan. Indeed the latter's treatise on the importance of naval power in international affairs was especially influential. Such voices fed what seemed to be an insatiable desire once again, manifesting itself in 1898 when America decided that it wanted control of Hawaii and took it—oddly not quite so differently as when Andrew Jackson took Florida nearly a century before. The supposed American mission to the islands came to fruition in 1959 when the United States made Hawaii its fiftieth state.[23]

Throughout American history the dual visions of the American people—of a divine providence destined by God to direct national expansion, or of a natural right to extend liberty (our own version, of course) to other parts of world—seemed to complement each other. Once again, it appeared that the means ultimately justified the end. As a people we embraced an unnamed, but not unknown, doctrine and made it our own. And, as in our previous history, we have taken concepts, ideologies, and policies—altering them to fit our own needs—and then applying them to our own country.

While this process is not totally detrimental, it hinders our ability to understand and examine American history as a part of world, as well as our own national, history. When faced

---

[23]Lubragge, "Manifest Destiny."

with attempting to understand the philosophy of destiny and the concept of being a "chosen people," it is most beneficial to widen our lens and focus on a broader picture. When this occurs, we can then understand that the United States did not create a new doctrine but simply embellished upon principles that can be traced back to earlier "chosen people" and their own individual views of natural right and nationalism. This philosophy began as far back—if not farther—as the Greek philosophy of Stoicism. Viewed that way, manifest destiny is a necessary requirement for all societies seeking a higher purpose for their own nation and peoples. This is not totally inconceivable since "all nations that are worth anything, always have had, and always will have, some ideal of national destiny, and without it, would soon disappear, and would deserve their fate."[24]

Bibliography

Adams, Ephraim Douglass. *The Power of Ideals in American History.* New York: AMS Press, Inc. 1969.

Barker, Ernest. *Traditions of Civility.* Cambridge: Cambridge University Press, 1948.

Haynes, Sam W. "Manifest Destiny." In The U.S. Mexican War (1846-1848). http://www.pbs. org/kera/usmexicanwar/prelude/md_manifest_ destiny.html. Updated 6 August 1999. Accessed 12 February 2011.

Horsman, Reginald. *Race and Manifest Destiny.* Cambridge: Harvard University Press. 1981.

LaFeber, Walter. "The World and the United States." *The American Historical Review* 100 (October 1995): 1015-1033.

---

[24]Adams, 68.

Long, A. A., ed. *Problems in Stoicism*. London: The Athlone Press. 1971.

Lubragge, Michael T. "Manifest Destiny: The Philosophy That Created a Nation." In From Revolution to Reconstruction. http://odur.let. rug.nl/~usa/E/manifest/manif1.htm. Updated 6 March 2003. Accessed 13 February 2011.

Merk, Frederick. *Manifest Destiny and Mission in American History, A Reinterpretation*. New York: Alfred A. Knopf, 1963.

O'Sullivan, John L. "Annexation." *Democratic Review* 17 (July and August 1845). In *Manifest Destiny and the Imperialism Question,* ed. Charles L. Sanford, 26–34. New York: John Wiley & Sons, 1974.

Pratt, Julius W. "The Origin of 'Manifest Destiny.'" *The American Historical Review* 32 (1927): 798.

Sanford, Charles L., ed. *Manifest Destiny and the Imperialism Question*. New York: John Wiley & Sons, Inc. 1974.

Tacitus, Publius Cornelius. *The Agricola and Germania,* trans. A. J. Church and W. J. Brodribb. London: Macmillan, 1877. In Medieval Source Book, ed. Paul Halsall. http://www.fordham.edu/halsall/source/tacitus1.html. January 1996. Accessed 30 April 2006.

Webb, Walter Prescott. "The Frontier and the 400 Year Boom." In *The Turner Thesis concerning the Role of the Frontier in American History,* ed. George Rogers Clark, 87–95. Boston: D. C. Heath and Company. 1956.

Weinberg, Albert K. *Manifest Destiny: A Study of Nationalist Expansionism in American History*. New York: Johns Hopkins Press. 1958.

THINGS TO NOTICE ABOUT THIS PAPER

This paper is more a historiographic essay than some traditional history papers. Nonetheless, it still presents primary sources, secondary sources, and the interpretations of the author to arrive at a thesis: Manifest Destiny was not just a phenomenon of American history. The paper is more than a mere collection of sources pasted together. The writer has thought about the material and has arrived at some interpretations that help explain it. She has inferred much from her sources and has treated some of the writings of philosophers and historians as primary sources, as she should.

The author's own point of view is unmistakable: She points out a long-standing interpretation of American history—one that has sometimes captured the popular imagination—and indicates how her interpretation differs. She identifies the source of the phrase and then traces the essential idea back through English history to its ancient roots. She arrives at a judgment about the effect of this on the history of the United States, but she does not preach to the reader. A historian can make judgments on whether certain ideas or actions in the past were good or bad. Historians do that sort of thing all the time. But it is not acceptable in the field of history to rage about events in the past as if your readers must be more persuaded by your emotions than by your evidence and your reasoning. Readers don't begin this paper to see how upset or self-righteous the writer is; they read to see how a fundamental idea about American history actually ties the United States into a broad reach of global history. You should trust your readers as Ms. Sonnenburg has trusted hers.

The paper is documented throughout so readers may look up the evidence should they want to know more about it. Notice particularly how Ms. Sonnenburg has used primary sources, some located on the Internet and others identified in the writings of others. This helps prevent the paper from being a collage of what other historians have written about manifest destiny. This technique is highly valuable, especially when you face limitations of direct access to the original primary sources. The thoughtfulness of the author in dealing with her sources is enough to make us feel that we have learned something important from someone who has taken pains to become an authority on an important aspect of U.S. history and see how it has larger historical implications.

Answer the questions that follow by studying this sample paper. You would do well to ask these questions about your own writing as well.

Writer's Checklist for Sample Research Paper

_____   ✔ What sentence or sentences near the beginning of the paper announce the writer's thesis, the main idea that controls the paper?

_____   ✔ How does the writer use quotations? Why does she use shorter quotations, rather than larger block quotations, throughout? Where does she seem to use paraphrase instead?

_____   ✔ What form do the footnotes take? Why does the form sometimes change?

_____   ✔ Where does the writer use secondary sources? Can you show where she disagrees with some of her secondary sources?

_____   ✔ Where does the author make inferences? That is, where does she make plausible suggestions about the meaning of various texts when the meaning is not explicit in the text itself?

_____   ✔ Which paragraphs in the essay are primarily narrative? Where does the author write in a more expository mode?

_____   ✔ Where are there arguments in the essay that are intended to persuade?

_____   ✔ Where does the writer make her own judgments clear?

_____   ✔ Where does the author use simile and metaphor to good effect?

_____   ✔ In what ways does the conclusion of the paper mirror some of the ideas in the opening?

APPENDIX B

■ ■ ■

Writing Reviews

Reviewing is an essential part of the historian's profession. Book reviews, as well as reviews of Web sites and other historical works, represent an assessment of the efforts of other historians. Writing reviews is also a good way to train yourself in understanding how the discipline of history works. Such writing is often complicated and demanding. Reviewers do report on the content of the book (or other type of presentation), but they also evaluate the work by discussing matters such as the author's logic and organization, evidence and conclusions, and sometimes even the writer's style of presentation.

REVIEWING AS A SPECIAL FORM OF WRITING

While writing a review does require many of the same writing skills we have discussed in this book, it is also a special form of historical writing. You are expected to engage with the historical ideas of another author, to report on and evaluate them, and to present your conclusions to other historians. Such an effort will draw you into debates about historical subjects. That is why many students are asked to write book reviews in their history classes. But keep in mind there are several types of reviews; for convenience, we refer to them as popular, academic, and scholastic reviews.

Popular reviews are generally written for publications having a general, but informed readership, such as *The Atlantic, Harper's, The New Republic, The New York Review,* or similar magazines. Some newspapers, such as the *New York Times* and the *Washington Post,* also carry similar reviews in some of their editions. Occasionally, popular reviews range far and wide, often extending beyond the contents of a book or other presentation to issues which it raises in the reviewer's mind. Thus, some popular reviews take the form of extended essays on particular subjects that may include the topic of the book, books, and any other materials under review or even occasionally narrower aspects of that topic. While these are frequently very interesting essays, they do not always offer very practical models for the types of reviews you may be asked to write.

Two other types of reviews are more important as guides to your own writing. The first, which we call *academic reviews,* usually appear in professional journals such as *The American Historical Review,* the *Journal of World History,* or *The Historian.* These are frequently much shorter than popular reviews—often little more than five hundred words—and are generally intended for a scholarly audience. On occasion, historical journals may also publish one or two longer "review essays," which more closely approximate what we have termed *popular reviews.* But for historians, these review essays frequently focus on the important scholarly issues raised by the book or books the reviewer is considering. We suggest that you look at the reviews, and review essays, in historical journals and also at the H-Net Reviews Web site, http://www.h-net.org/reviews; these will give you some idea of the way historians generally prepare and present reviews.

Reviews you may be asked to write in one or more of your courses should bear some similarities to the following example; we refer to these class assignments as *scholastic reviews.* They are generally longer than most academic reviews but are also intended for a more scholarly audience—your instructors and fellow students. In some ways, they are much more like the *review essays* we mentioned previously, which sometimes appear in scholarly journals. Your instructor may provide very specific instructions about what should appear in such a review; if so, heed them. But here are some general guidelines that should help you in writing better book reviews no matter what your specific instructions may be.

1. **Read the book!** That may seem self-evident, but it remains perhaps the most important advice about writing a review. Now and then even professional historians do not read the books they review in journals. You can see their errors when outraged authors

write to protest; occasionally you will find such communications in historical journals. Don't let that happen to you! If you find and read one or more academic reviews of a book you have been assigned or have selected to review, you may learn a great deal. But that is *not* a substitute for reading the book and making your own judgments. Also remember this: Fundamental honesty requires for you to say if you take something—ideas or quotations—for your book review from a review someone else has written. Our cautions about paraphrase (and plagiarism) in Chapter 1 apply to your reviews as well!

2. **Identify the author, but don't waste time on needless or extravagant claims.** It is a cliché to say that the author is "well qualified" to write a book; such a comment adds little to your review. You may write briefly about the author's background and perhaps the work done in creating a book you are reviewing. But don't belabor the point; two or three sentences are usually sufficient.

3. **Always give the author's major theme or thesis, the motive for writing the book.** What is your assessment of that theme or thesis? Read the book thoughtfully. Always read the introduction or the preface. Students in a hurry may skip the introduction, thinking they are saving time. That can be a serious mistake. Authors often use introductions to state the reasons that impelled them to write their books. Indeed, we recommend you read the preface, the introduction, and the last chapter of a book before you read the complete work. Few writers can bear to leave their books without a parting shot; they want to be sure readers get the point! Reviewers should take advantage of that impulse.

   Some of our students object to our advice that they read the last chapter first. We remind them that history books are not novels, and good history books—as well as shorter essays—almost never have surprise endings. By reading the last chapter, you see where the author is heading as you read the entire book. And always remember the *theme* and *thesis* are not quite the same thing as the subject. The subject of the book may be the biography of Winston Churchill, prime minister of Great Britain during World War II. The theme or thesis, however, may be that Churchill was a great wartime leader but a poor interpreter of the postwar world.

4. **Summarize, but only briefly, the evidence the author presents in support of the thesis.** Do not fall into the habit of writing a

summary of the book as if you were writing a report rather than a review. This approach seldom can be translated into a successful book *review*. Don't try to report every interesting detail in the book. Leave something for readers to discover on their own. But it frequently is a good idea to recount some interesting incidents. Tell a story or two from the book. You would also do well to consider the types of evidence the author has used and particularly the effort to rely on primary sources.

5. **Consider quoting a line or two here and there in your review to give the flavor of the text.** Quote selectively but fairly. The prose of the author you review may help spice up your own review, but avoid long chunks of quotation. You must show your readers that you have absorbed the book you review and that you understand it sufficiently to describe the author's ideas in your own words.

6. **Avoid lengthy comments about the style of the presentation.** It is fine to say that the style is good, bad, interesting, or tedious. If a book is especially well written or if it is incomprehensible, you may quote a sentence to illustrate a good or bad style, but don't belabor the point. Generalizations such as, "This book is interesting," or "This book is boring," do little to enhance your review. If you do your job in the review, readers can tell whether you find it interesting or boring. And remember, if you are bored, the fault might be in you rather than the book. An Ancient History professor at the University of Tennessee, when one of us said reading the Greek philosopher Plutarch was boring, declared sternly, "Mr. Marius, you have no right to be bored with Plutarch." Both of us agree the instructor was right.

7. **Don't feel compelled to say negative things about the book.** If you find inaccuracies, say so. If you disagree with the writer's interpretation here and there, say that, too, giving your reasons. However, you should avoid passionate attacks on the book. Scholarship is not always courteous, but it should be. Reviewers who launch savage attacks usually make fools of themselves. Remember, too, that petty complaints about a book may also make you look foolish or unfair. Do not waste time pointing out minor errors unless they change the meaning the author intends. Always remember that every good historical work has flaws. The author may make some minor errors in fact or some questionable judgments. Even so, a book may be extremely valuable.

Don't condemn outright because you find some mistakes. Try to judge a book or other historical presentation as a whole.

8. **Review what the author has presented.** You may wish an author had written a different book. You might write a different book yourself. But the author has written *this* book. If the book did not need to be written, if it adds nothing to our knowledge of the field, if it makes conclusions unwarranted by the evidence, say so. But don't review the book as if it should be another book.

9. **Try to bring something from your own experience—your reading, your recollections, your thoughts, your reflections—to your review.** If you are reviewing a book about twentieth-century China, and if you have been fortunate enough to have traveled in China, you may bring your own impressions to your review. Try to make use of a broad part of your education when you write a review. If you have read books in other classes that are relevant to a particular class for which you are writing the review, say something about those other books in your review. If you know facts the author has overlooked, say so. But avoid writing as if you possess independent knowledge of the author's subject when in fact you have taken all you know from the book itself. Don't pretend to be an expert when you are not. Be honest.

A Sample Student Review

The following review, of Thomas Fleming's *Washington's Secret War: The Hidden History of Valley Forge,* was written by one of our students, Brandy Arnall. Read her review carefully, considering some of our previous suggestions for writing your own reviews.

Thomas Fleming's Discovery of Another War

A Review of Thomas Fleming, *Washington's Secret War:*
The Hidden History of Valley Forge

BY BRANDY TAYLOR ARNALL
East Tennessee State University
April 17, 2008
History 3410: Historical Methods
Professor Melvin E. Page

Thomas Fleming's 2005 book, *Washington's Secret War: The Hidden History of Valley Forge,* is an updated and eye-opening account of General George Washington and Valley Forge. Washington has often been oversimplified as the long-suffering general who did nothing during the winter of 1777-1778 at Valley Forge but grieve the condition of his army in letters to various state governors and congressmen of the Continental government. According to Fleming during his research about Valley Forge, he surprisingly discovered a new side of George Washington:

> This Washington was not the long-suffering general who did little in the six months at Valley Forge but bemoan the condition of his starving ... army in letters.... He was a man who confronted not only the threat of his army's collapse, he also resisted the ruin of his reputation as a leader and a patriot, and struck back at his enemies with ferocity and guile. (xii)

Fleming argues in his book that General Washington was a politician and a very good one. The author offers proof for this argument by providing information on which people were Washington's enemies, their motives, and how the general responded to various attacks, all the while commanding his troops at Valley Forge. Fleming also provides examples of those who were Washington supporters and how he used this support to his advantage.

A widely published author, Fleming is equally skilled in writing novels as well as historical studies, some of the latter commissioned by the National Park Service. Most of his works, both fiction and nonfiction, concern aspects of the military in the history of the United States and include an earlier biography of Washington, *First in Their Hearts* (1984). His fascination with true stories of the American past is clear in his admission that he "reached one undebatable conclusion: history is full of surprises" (xi).

The main surprise Fleming relates in this book is not only that Washington had enemies but so many, and that they consisted of leading officers in the Continental Army and the Continental Congress! His account of General Washington is not the simple narrative that older generations are familiar with, but it is one that puts to use evidence gathered from previously unstudied letters and diaries. From this research Fleming has identified Washington's major opponents during the time at Valley Forge. The list of Washington's enemies includes but is not limited to General Horatio Gates, Colonel Thomas Conway, Quartermaster General Thomas Mifflin, and Samuel Adams.

This book describes Washington's battles with Gates, Conway, and Mifflin as ones that involved the three in ambitious struggles for self-promotion and power, especially Gates. The three men formed what can be described as an alliance in their efforts. While Washington and the army took winter quarters at Valley Forge, their main objective seemed to be centered on making General Washington look like a fool who was responsible for the adverse conditions happening to the Continental Army. These three enemies of Washington always seemed to try to work against him in an "underground" fashion in order to protect themselves if ever called upon to answer for their actions. Fleming's work on this matter describes what each of these men's jobs were in the Continental Army and how they each failed to measure up to the excellent standard required of them. Oftentimes, as Fleming shows his readers, these men intentionally fell short of the standard required because of pride and jealousies against Washington. Fleming does an excellent job of providing examples of such shortcomings. One such example of falling short is that of Gate's victory at Saratoga. According to research done by Fleming in letters and war records, Gates never notified General Washington of the victory. This showed not only indifference to the commander in chief but also disrespect.

These men not only fell short of their duties and tried to blame Washington, but they also participated in negative conversations with one another about the general. One prime example that Fleming provides is a letter from Conway to Mifflin in which Washington is described as a weak general with bad counselors who would ruin everything if it were not for "Heaven" being "determined to save the country" (116). As word of this opinion became available to Washington, Gates and Conway did everything they each could do to make themselves look innocent. These of course are only two examples in Fleming's book, that provide far greater detailed information on all the actions these men took against Washington; it is worth reading to learn more!

The next man in this secret war against Washington was Samuel Adams. In reality Samuel Adams was not only one enemy but a multitude of enemies that he brought with him from the New England states. Adams and his supporters considered themselves "True Whigs" and clashed with Washington on a number of philosophical issues including the definition of patriotism in the American Revolution. The New Englanders carried an extreme belief that soldiers and Americans should only be motivated by the love of liberty and participate in the Revolution simply on this belief. Washington, however, realized that even a person motivated by liberty had economic needs that needed to be met eventually. Fleming's insights into Washington's battle with these New Englanders provide an often overlooked aspect of the American Revolution.

In these and other examples, Fleming makes use of compelling research that shows Washington's handling of all of these examples, and many more, in his book. This is how Fleming provides proof for his thesis that Washington was a skilled politician. It is important to note that this review only highlights a few of the adversities Washington confronted while commander in chief, but Fleming shows throughout each of Washington's trials that he handled it all with a collective calmness. The author shows that Washington's main goal through it all was never to let the public learn of any growing disunity between those who called themselves Patriots. Fleming feels that Washington understood that it was not only harmful for the British to see factions forming but also for the bulk of Americans who were not committed or only half-heartedly committed to the Revolution. Throughout this book Fleming shows that Washington possessed a great understanding of what was taking place around him at all times and knew how to handle things for the benefit of the American cause.

By presenting these examples of who was doing what to discredit Washington, and how the general dealt with these attempts, Fleming succeeds at giving credible evidence to his thesis and makes this book a successful attempt in teaching history. The author also proves his point about Washington in a highly enjoyable read that involves sections broken down into easily read storytelling instead of dry lists of evidence. In *Washington's Secret War* Fleming does go into great detail in chapters two and nine about the British and easy life in Philadelphia with almost no mention of Washington and the "secret war." It seems that Fleming provided information about the British and the extravagant lifestyles in Philadelphia to provide a dramatic contrast to what Washington was dealing with secretly on top of what was happening during the winter at Valley Forge. The author's approach in these two chapters is understandable but can cause frustration to the eagerly curious reader who wants to dive right into the "secret war" and stay in it. However, this is a minor criticism that should not outweigh the value of Fleming's work in this book.

Another positive note about *Washington's Secret War* is that between pages eighty-two and eighty-three is a set of pictures of prominent Washington enemies with captions explaining such things as who is in the picture, army title or congressional title, and what the person did in participating in the "secret war" against the

commander in chief. Also in this set are pictures
of some of Washington's most helpful allies
with information on what they did to support
the general. It is important to note that Fleming includes these supporters in the text of his
book and shows how each played a role in helping
Washington in the battles secretly waged against
him. It is yet another surprise that the author
puts into this book that makes it worth reading.
Another helpful feature of this book is the Notes
section, which is neatly organized and makes checking Fleming's sources easy. Fleming's well-docu-
mented notes also give credibility to his research
in producing *Washington's Secret War* and provides a
starting point for readers who want more information about this topic.

Overall, Fleming's well-written book presents
a refreshing view of General George Washington that
debunks many myths about the man and Valley Forge.
This book is for readers interested in and dedicated to what some have labeled "telling the truth
about history." Fleming makes an effort to provide
a more honest view of who Washington actually was
and how things were in reality taking place during
the American Revolution. This is not the story
where absolutely everyone loved Washington and all
Americans were sacrificing for an "American Cause."
Fleming shows the very human side of the Revolution
by revealing the secret war Washington dealt with.
For these reasons, I would highly recommend this
book to other students of history.

THINGS TO NOTICE ABOUT THIS REVIEW

How does this review measure up to the guidelines that precede it? Does it seem to miss any of them, and if so, does that detract from the review? In what ways is this a review rather than a report about the book? What impressions of the book are you left with after reading this review? Are there any unanswered questions which might keep you from reading the book? Or would you look for this book the next time you wanted to find more information on the general topic it considers, the American Revolution?

As you think about these issues and the review you have just read, also consider how you would go about reviewing a book (or other historical presentation) the next time you are asked to do so. You can also use the following checklist as a guide in preparing your own review.

Writer's Checklist for Reviews

_____ ✔ Does my review give evidence that I read the book?

_____ ✔ Have I adequately identified the main theme or thesis?

_____ ✔ Are my explanations of both the evidence and the argument used to support the central thesis clear?

_____ ✔ Have I appropriately considered the writing style of the author?

_____ ✔ Are my judgments of the author's work both temperate and sound?

_____ ✔ Have I reviewed what the author has written and presented?

_____ ✔ Was I able to bring something personal to my review?

APPENDIX C

■ ■ ■

Short Essay Assignments

In many history courses you may be asked to write short essays, often on very specific topics. For example, we frequently ask our students to write short essays—usually no more than about five hundred words (or two printed pages)—about a portion of a reading we have assigned for a course. These essays, and many similar assignments, are intended to encourage thoughtful reading of some document, historical essay, or even a journal article and to stimulate careful consideration of it in a written essay. Often such assignments are made well in advance so you may plan your reading and studying accordingly. Sometimes they may be announced just prior to your reading or studying the material about which you are expected to write. On other occasions, very similar questions may be the basis for essay examinations, requiring you to reflect seriously on what you have been studying.

One such advanced notice assignment we have used is based on students reading an excerpt from the royal chronicle of the Christian monarch Amda Seyon, who ruled Ethiopia from 1314 to 1344. We ask students to write a five-hundred-word essay comparing Amda Seyon's efforts in resisting Islamic invasions to similar situations in Europe and elsewhere at about the same time. In another assignment, sometimes introduced in class as an immediate prelude to discussion, we invite students to study the famous Jan van Eych painting of 1434, *Giovanni Arnolfini and His Bride*. Then we ask them to write a short essay about the objects van Eych depicts and how they offer evidence concerning the social standing of merchants in medieval Europe.[1]

These brief essays are somewhat different from other kinds of (usually longer) essays we have discussed in this book. They are actually more like essay examinations, to be written within a given time in circumstances where you must rely on your memory, usually without the aid of notes, books, the reference room of a library, or the Internet. Essay exams test what you know and how you think about what you know. They are to some degree artificial creations; historians usually do not write under the strictures of the standard essay exam format. They write and revise, go back to their sources, and revise some more. So essay exams frequently are the most comprehensive test of how much you have learned in a history course. They are so much a part of the Western academic scene that you doubtless already have much experience with them. The best examinations allow you to show your knowledge about the facts, demonstrate some recall of sources for these facts, and prove that you can make judgments about them.

Perhaps the best way to prepare to write any of these short essays, including exams, is to study the readings you have been assigned, attend class diligently, and take good notes. The best way to take notes—from classes or readings—is to jot down important concepts using key words and phrases using your mobile device or a paper notepad. As soon as you can after class or a period of reading, review what you initially recorded and using these original notes as your foundation, write out an account of what the professor said or what you read, perhaps on a separate computer file. When something is unclear, ask what the point was; use reference books, and especially your textbooks, to make sure you understand the information. All this takes time, of course, and college students are busy, many of them working at jobs to support themselves in school. It is hard to take the time to go over notes shortly after taking them. Yet if you force yourself to do so, you will discover that you may save time in the long run.

Making a habit of reviewing your class and reading notes will impress the information on your brain. You will become acquainted with your own

---

[1]Copies of both these documents and introductory discussions of each can be found in Dennis Sherman et al., *World Civilizations: Sources, Images, and Interpretations*, 3rd ed. (New York: McGraw-Hill, 2002), 230–231, 243–244.

notes, and when time for writing a short essay assignment or taking an essay exam draws near, you can face it without cramming just ahead of time. You'll already know most of the material! You might get together with classmates and come up with a collection of class notes—from lectures and your reading—that you have all cooperated in putting together. In our experience, students who study together and talk about the class are more likely to make the highest grades on their essays. In our opinion, this is not deceitful, but rather a reflection of the cooperative spirit of much historical work.

If you receive the question for a short essay ahead of time, study it. If you only receive the question shortly before you begin to write, you can still be prepared for what questions you do receive. Pay particular attention to what your professor emphasizes in class. Try to think what questions you would ask if you were that professor. Remember, professors usually believe that if they have spent a long time discussing a subject in class, it's only fair to expect students to know something about it! If you write out questions of your own, you will be surprised at how well you sometimes can read your professor's mind. Once you have the question for your essay, follow the directions carefully. *Read the questions.* We have always been surprised at how often students will read questions carelessly and write an essay having almost nothing to do with the topic.

In looking at the questions, determine what mode of historical writing each of them calls for. Your primary task may be to tell a story: "Trace the career of Martin Luther from the Indulgence Controversy of 1517 to his appearance before the Diet of Worms in 1521." You will need to narrate a sequence of events from 1517 to 1521, being careful to choose the most important steps in this part of Luther's career. Or you may be asked to explain the historical significance of an event, a document, or a person: "Discuss the significance of the heroic image of Sun Yat-sen in the developing ideologies of Chinese Communism and its 'Nationalist' opponents." To answer this question you must prepare an exposition that will first explain the "heroic image" of Sun Yat-sen as he became the leader in the effort to free the Chinese from European imperialist control. Then you will need to tell what his program for China included and how it changed as first the Communists under Mao Zedong and then the rival Kuomintang party under Chiang Kai-shek took over his message for their own ends. You can complete your exposition by indicating why and how these changes were significant in China's history.

Related to questions about significance are comparison questions, which many history professors are fond of asking. In effect, the professor gets two answers from you for the price of one question! And you are required to demonstrate the flexibility of your mind and the quantity of your knowledge about two portions of the course material. For example: "Compare Thomas More's *Utopia* and Machiavelli's *The Prince,* both written in 1516." Again, you will need to write an exposition, in this case one which explains the key ideas in both books, recognizing that both More and Machiavelli were preoccupied with reform. You will also want to emphasize that there were differences in the kind of reform each wanted. And you can conclude by evaluating how each reform program affected the world of medieval Europe. In making this comparison you can, in addition, explain how radically different two people, living at the same time in similar cultures, can be.

Other short essay questions may ask that you argue a point and persuade your professor of your command of the information. These essays are difficult and challenging. You might be given a question such as this: "Which African national leader of the 1960s provided the best program of government for his nation in the two decades following its independence from colonial control? What arguments would you make to support your choice?" Whether you select Kwame Nkrumah, Julius Nyerere, or another African leader, you would need to construct your essay making a plausible case for whomever you decide to write about. But remember, historians seldom prove anything beyond any doubt. You cannot resolve every uncertainty and eliminate all contrary opinions in the limited space you have for a short essay, and certainly not in the few minutes you have to write an examination. You can, however, show that you know the material, have thought about it intelligently, and can offer a cogent rationale for what it means. As always in making your argument, you should show some familiarity with viewpoints contrary to your own and provide a few words about why you reject them.

Among our favorite short essay questions are those asking students to analyze an important text. Your professor may give you a paragraph from a noteworthy historical document and ask you to write about what it means. Such questions could also be more focused than that. One question that we recently posed for students was this:

> The European philosopher Francis Bacon observed in the early seventeenth century that "the force and virtue and consequences of discoveries ... are to be seen nowhere more conspicuously than these three which were unknown to the

ancients ... namely, printing, gunpowder, and the
compass. For these have changed the whole face and
state of things throughout the world." Would you
agree with Bacon that the development and spread of
these technological innovations had such a profound
impact on world history?

This question not only requires a student to think carefully about
some very specific things, but it also demands consideration of their significance. One of our students, Bill Hembrock, wrote a short essay answering
this question in a recent examination for a course on *World History to 1500:*

All three of these discoveries were brought
to the West from China where they had been invented during the Tang and Song dynasties. Once known
there, they played a significant role in advancing
Europe's power around the globe after 1500, just as
Bacon suggested.

The gunpowder chemistry originally developed
in China was not a very effective military weap-
on. It was brought to the West with the Mongol
conquerors, as Bentley and Ziegler describe in
Traditions & Encounters [the course textbook],
where the technology was refined and the first
crude cannons were used in battle. Later sailors
and explorers from Europe were able to advance
the technology to assist in conquering people in
their explorations and empire building, such as
the Portuguese in Africa; the Spanish in Central,
South, and North America; and the British in India.

The magnetic compass was also invented in China
but, as the text also points out, was spread first
throughout the Indian Ocean by Indian and African
sailors who used the compass and the trade winds
to facilitate a great deal of trade throughout the
Indian Ocean, from northern Africa, eastern Africa,
and India on to southeast Asia and China. Eventually the knowledge got to the European navigators,
who used it to explore the rest of the oceans of
the world and finally tie the whole world together.
From then on trade and exchange of ideas, diseases,
customs, and religions could be exchanged from anywhere in the world to any other part of the globe.

Printing, the text again notes, was invented in China, but taken from its Asian roots and
advanced by Europeans. Printing helped agricul-
ture improve in Europe in the thirteenth through
fifteenth centuries by spreading information
about new techniques on raising different crops.
The printing of the Bible also helped spread the
faith and unify the Christian world. Europe was
united by Christianity, with the church exerting
great authority over the people through scriptural
authority, common beliefs, and church practices.

Europe had been a fractured area politically
and backward compared to other great empires of the
world especially after the collapse of the Roman
Empire. By taking these three inventions and adapt-
ing them for their needs and advancement, European
countries became the discoverers and great empires
of the post-1500 world.

Notice how the author begins with a short paragraph offering a thesis statement which refers specifically to the text quoted within the question. He follows this with separate paragraphs on each of the three discoveries Bacon mentions, analyzing the significance of each. And he concludes his argument by referring again to his thesis. He also mentions the textbook assigned for the course, where he found much of his information; this is much the same as the citations to sources you would provide in a longer essay.

Achieving this balance in any short essay requires study and preparation in advance, and then careful planning when you first receive the question. We encourage students to jot down quickly words and phrases they remember concerning the question, and then to reorganize that collage of ideas into a basic outline. For an examination especially, you must do this quickly and also carefully judge how much time you can spend on each part of an examination. Take care not to spend too much of your time organizing—or on writing one part of an essay or answering only one of several questions asked on an exam. After completing your college education, you will discover that allocating time is one of the most essential tasks of a human being; efficient use of time in writing examination essays is good training for what will come later on.

Managing your time and the space available is, of course, an important part of writing any history essay. Yet even in a very short essay, whether or not during an exam, you need to be as specific as possible. You must name people, dates, documents, places—answering the basic historian's questions: *Who? What? When? Where? Why?* These questions should haunt your mind, and you should always be trying to answer them as you read and write. Plan your work carefully to be certain you can complete those tasks. Doing so will help you prepare to answer any history question. You likely will discover that time spent considering them—even before you know what questions you may need to write about—offers you an opportunity to shape your knowledge, integrate various parts of it, and produce an essay (even on an examination!) that may be not only a source of pleasure but also of pride.

As you complete any short history essay, including those you may write for an essay examination, read over what you have written before you submit it. Take enough time to consider the key questions in the "Writer's Checklist for Short Essays" that follows.

Writer's Checklist for Short Essays

_____ ✔ Have I sharply focused my topic?
_____ ✔ Have I made a clearly stated argument?
_____ ✔ Have I carefully acknowledged the sources of ideas and evidence?
_____ ✔ Have I included my own original thoughts?
_____ ✔ Have I expressed myself clearly?

SELECT BIBLIOGRAPHY OF STUDENT RESOURCES

■ ■ ■

Appleby, Joyce, Lynn Hunt, and Margaret Jacob. *Telling the Truth About History.* New York: W. W. Norton, 1995.

> A challenging and sometimes provocative consideration of developments in historical thinking and practice, especially in the United States at the end of the twentieth century.

Arnold, John. *History: A Very Short Introduction.* Oxford and New York: Oxford University Press, 2000.

> This book offers short yet thoughtful considerations of a few very basic issues confronting historians as they write about the past.

Barzun, Jacques. *On Writing, Editing, and Publishing: Essays Explicative and Hortatory,* 2nd ed. Chicago: University of Chicago Press, 1986.

> A collection of essays written between 1950 and 1985 by American historian Jacques Barzun, including consideration of "A Writer's Discipline" (pp. 5–17).

———. *Simple and Direct: A Rhetoric for Writers,* 4th ed. New York: Quill, 2001.

> A somewhat philosophical approach to writing with excellent suggestions from an accomplished historian and writer.

Barzun, Jacques, and Henry F. Graff. *The Modern Researcher,* 6th ed. Belmont, CA: Wadsworth/Thompson Learning, 2004.

> For half a century, the advice of these distinguished American historians has guided many history students as well as an informed and curious public in the craft of telling stories about the past intended to be true.

Berger, Stefan, Heiko Feldner, and Kevin Passmore, eds. *Writing History: Theory and Practice.* London: Arnold, 2003.

> Sixteen essays examine problems, issues, and examples some historians have encountered when writing about history.

Brundage, Anthony. *Going to the Sources: A Guide to Historical Research and Writing,* 4th ed. Wheeling, IL: Harlan Davidson, 2007.

Nearly twenty percent of this very brief guide is taken up with an excellent treatment of writing a historiographic essay, including a sample student effort.

Burrow, John. *A History of Histories: Epics, Chronicles, and Inquiries from Herodotus and Thucydides to the Twentieth Century.* New York: Vintage Books, 2009.

An eloquent appreciation of historical literature in the Western tradition over many centuries by a distinguished British historian.

Donnelly, Mark and Claire Norton. *Doing History.* London and New York: Routledge, 2011.

Written expressly for students just beginning a formal study of history, this book focuses primarily on how the practice of historians and the histories they write have changed even in the past quarter century.

Feinstein, Charles H. and Mark Thomas. *Making History Count: A Primer in Quantitative Methods for Historians.* New York: Cambridge University Press, 2002.

This book is considered by some historians to be the best introduction to the subject for their discipline and therefore highly recommended for students.

Gaddis, John Lewis. *The Landscape of History: How Historians Map the Past.* New York: Oxford University Press, 2002.

Contends that the modern practice of history is more akin to new scientific fields, such as geology and evolutionary biology, than the social and political sciences.

Gilderhus, Mark T. *History and Historians: A Historiographical Introduction,* 7th ed. Upper Saddle River, NJ: Pearson Prentice Hall, 2009.

An excellent brief introduction to the development of historical thinking in the Western tradition. Provides a good background for understanding historical theory and research methodologies.

Grafton, Anthony. *The Footnote: A Curious History,* rev. ed. Cambridge, MA: Harvard University Press, 1999.

An engaging history of scholarly attribution by a distinguished American historian, emphasizing the ways in which "footnotes" also constitute a means of historical conversation.

Hughes-Warrington, Marnie. *Fifty Key Thinkers on History,* 2nd ed. London and New York: Routledge, 2008.

These brief intellectual biographies offer a guide to the practice of history from ancient times until the present, although forty percent of the historians considered were born in the twentieth century.

Lukacs, John. *A Student's Guide to the Study of History.* Wilmington, DE: ISI Books, 2000.

Written by a distinguished, culturally conservative historian, this is only a brief overview of the discipline and its attractions.

MacMillan, Margaret. *Dangerous Games: The Uses and Abuses of History.* New York: Modern Library, 2010.

An accomplished Anglo-Canadian historian offers an analysis of many recent problems—even scandals—in the presentation of historical knowledge; particularly useful because of the extensive European, North American, and other appropriate examples.

Marwick, Arthur. *The New Nature of History: Knowledge, Evidence, Language.* Chicago: Lyceum Books, 2001.

Thirty years after preparing a guide to *The Nature of History,* a prolific British historian reflects on the changes in the practice and writing of history.

McMichael, Andrew. *History on the Web.* Wheeling, IL: Harlan Davidson, 2005.

A brief and basic introduction that nonetheless is a good touchstone even for those who believe they know how to use the Internet for historical research.

Munslow, Alun. *History of History.* London and New York: Routledge, 2012.

Although focusing primarily on American and European historical study over the past three centuries, the essential argument is that what historians see as the "nature of history" itself has a variable history.

_____. *The Routledge Companion to Historical Studies,* 2nd ed. London and New York: Routledge, 2012.

A twenty-first-century perspective expanded with nearly ninety entries on many key topics of interest to beginning historians; includes an extensive bibliography keyed to the entries.

Perrin, Robert. *Pocket Guide to the Chicago Manual of Style.* Boston: Houghton Mifflin, 2007

Most valuable is section 8, "Preparing Note Forms for Electronic Sources," which consolidates advice on many key topics regarding electronic source citation from the fifteenth edition of *The Chicago Manual of Style.*

Posner, Richard A. *The Little Book of Plagiarism.* New York: Pantheon Books, 2007.

A U.S. federal judge and widely published author considers not only the basic legal principles underscoring plagiarism conventions but some very public examples and temptations for students as well.

Presnell, Jenny. *The Information-Literate Historian,* 2nd ed. New York: Oxford University Press, 2012.

Practical and sometimes detailed advice concerning historical research for students from an information services librarian and experienced instructor.

Southgate, Beverley. *What Is History For?* New York and London: Routledge, 2005.

A senior British historian examines the uses of history, with examples from the past as well as suggestions for future directions in historical writing.

Staley, David J. *Computers, Visualization, and History: How New Technology Will Transform Our Understanding of the Past*, 2nd ed.. Armonk, NY: M. E. Sharpe, 2014.

> Based on a sympathetic understanding of the potential that new technologies have to influence the presentation of historical knowledge, this book challenges readers with new insights on the treatment of the past.

Strunk, William, Jr. and E. B. White. *The Elements of Style,* 50th anniversary ed. New York: Longman, 2008.

> The justly famous "little book" with excellent tips about clear writing, brought up to date for the twenty-first century; this edition has details of the book's history.

Turabian, Kate L. *A Manual for Writers of Research Papers, Theses, and Dissertations*, 8th ed. Chicago: University of Chicago Press, 2013.

> This venerable guide for student writing, based on *The Chicago Manual of Style*, provides essential advice on research and writing as well as valuable guidance for making clear citations to sources in the notes-bibliography style most widely favored by historians.

Williams, Robert C. *The Forensic Historian: Using Science to Reexamine the Past.* Armonk, NY and London: M. E. Sharpe, 2013.

> A fascinating look at how some historians have turned to pathology, DNA testing, chemistry, and other sciences to solve historical puzzles.

Wilson, Norman J. *History in Crisis? Recent Directions in Historiography,* 3rd ed. Upper Saddle River, NJ: Pearson Education, 2013.

> A succinct consideration of many different approaches to historical study, with an emphasis on late-twentieth- and twenty-first-century controversies and debates among historians.

CREDITS

■ ■ ■

Page 9: Charles Ambler. Excerpt from "Popular Films and Colonial Audiences: The Movies in Northern Rhodesia" by Charles Ambler from *The American Historical Review*, vol. 106 (2001): 81–82, New York, NY: Oxford University Press, 2001. Page 23: Peter Charles Hoffer. Excerpt from "Reflections on Plagiarism—Part 1: 'A Guide for the Perplexed'" by Peter Charles Hoffer from *Perspectives: Newsmagazine of the American Historical Association*, vol. 42, no. 2 (February 2004): 19, Washington, DC: American Historical Association, 2004.

Pages 23–24: Jerry H. Bentley. Excerpt from *Old World Encounters* by Jerry H. Bentley. New York, NY: Oxford University Press, 1993.

Pages 38–39: Alfred W. Crosby. Excerpt from *Ecological Imperialism: The Biological Expansion of Europe* by Alfred W. Crosby, New York, NY: Cambridge University Press, 1986.

Page 74: Richard Hofstadter. Excerpt from *The Progressive Historians* by Richard Hofstadter, New York, NY: Alfred Knopf, a division of Random House, Inc., © 1968.

Pages 77–78: Sydney Mintz. Excerpt from *Sweetness and Power: The Place of Sugar in Modern History* by Sydney Mintz, London, UK: Penguin Books Ltd., © 1985.

Page 96: Jeff Jeske. Excerpt from "Two Types of Feedback" from "Peer Editing" in *Guilford College Writing Manual* by Jeff Jeske, Greensboro, NC: Guilford College, 2013.

Pages 98–99: Barbara W. Tuchman. Excerpt from *Practicing History* by Barbara W. Tuchman, New York, NY: Alfred A. Knopf, a division of Random House, Inc., 1982.

Page 102: Jonathan D. Spence. Excerpt from *The Death of Woman Wang* by Jonathan D. Spence, New York, NY: Viking Press, Penguin Group (USA), 1978.

Page 106: Margaret H. Darrow. Excerpt from "French Volunteer Nursing and the Myth of War Experience in World War I" by Margaret H. Darrow from *The American Historical Review*, vol. 101, no. 1, Feb. 1996, pp. 80-106, Washington, DC: American Historical Association, 1996.

INDEX

■ ■ ■